YOUTUBE FOR AUTHORS

HOW TO USE VIDEO TO SELL MORE
BOOKS AND BUILD YOUR BRAND

DALE L. ROBERTS

YouTube for Authors: How to Use Video to Sell More Books and Build Your Brand

All rights reserved.

Copyright ©2025 One Jacked Monkey, LLC

- Ebook ISBN: 978-1-63925-068-4
- Paperback ISBN: 978-1-63925-069-1
- Hardcover ISBN: 978-1-63925-070-7
- Audiobook ISBN: 978-1-63925-071-4

No part of this book may be reproduced in any form by any electronic or mechanical means, including information storage and retrieval systems, without permission in writing from the copyright owner, except by a reviewer who may quote brief passages in a review.

Disclaimer

The information provided in this book is accurate to the best of the author's knowledge at the time of publication. However, because of the evolving nature of the topics discussed, some information may change over time. The author makes no representations or warranties regarding the accuracy or completeness of the information contained within this book. It is the reader's responsibility to verify any facts or details, and to conduct further research or consult updated sources as needed.

Some recommended links in this book are part of affiliate programs. If you purchase a product through one of the links, then I get a portion of each sale. It doesn't affect your cost and greatly helps support the cause. If you have any reservations about buying a product through my affiliate link, then Google a direct link and bypass the affiliate link.

TABLE OF CONTENTS

INTRODUCTION:
    FROM ACCIDENTAL YOUTUBER TO AUTHOR SUCCESS STORY 1

CHAPTER 1:
    GETTING STARTED WITH YOUTUBE 8

CHAPTER 2:
    PLANNING YOUR FIRST VIDEOS 21

CHAPTER 3:
    CREATING VIDEOS THAT KEEP PEOPLE WATCHING 38

CHAPTER 4:
    GETTING DISCOVERED - YOUTUBE SEO THAT ACTUALLY WORKS 58

CHAPTER 5:
    BUILDING A LOYAL AUDIENCE AND ENGAGED COMMUNITY 76

CHAPTER 6:
    CONVERTING VIEWERS INTO READERS & BOOK BUYERS 90

CHAPTER 7:
    MONETIZING YOUR CHANNEL WITHOUT SELLING OUT 105

CHAPTER 8:
> OPTIMIZING YOUR CHANNEL FOR GROWTH & DISCOVERABILITY 122

CHAPTER 9:
> ADVANCED STRATEGIES TO ACCELERATE CHANNEL GROWTH 135

CHAPTER 10:
> SUSTAINING SUCCESS & PLANNING FOR LONG-TERM GROWTH 143

CONCLUSION:
> LIVING THE DREAM—FROM VHS TAPES TO GLOBAL REACH 152

A SMALL ASK... 156
ABOUT THE AUTHOR 157
SPECIAL THANKS 160
RESOURCES 161
REFERENCES 164

WANT A PROVEN PATH TO A STRONG BOOK LAUNCH?

Get my free **Bestseller Book Launch Checklist** and weekly insider tips to help you sell more books.

Grab yours at

DaleLinks.com/Checklist

> "I've used dozens of book cover design services over the last ten years, and none compare to the level of quality and professionalism that Miblart delivers."
>
> — *Dale L. Roberts*

Miblart - a book cover design company for self-published authors

Designers who specialize in different genres	Unlimited number of revisions
No deposit to get started	You can pay in installments

GET A BOOK COVER THAT WILL BECOME YOUR N°1 MARKETING TOOL

Excellent

 4.9

Your Book Marketing & YouTube Companion

Meet **Dibbly Create.**

Your All-in-1 A.I. companion for writing, publishing & marketing your book.

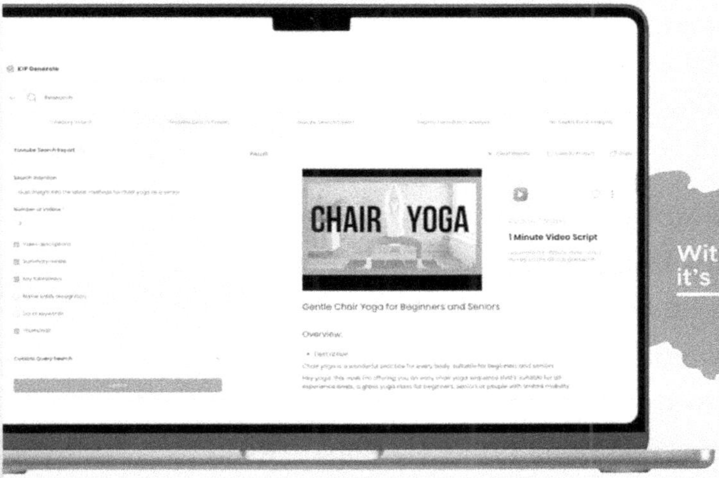

With Dibbly, it's done.

Yes,
I Need Help Marketing my Book

A.I. Assisted:

- ✓ YouTube Research
- ✓ YouTube Video Script
- ✓ Audience Engagement
- ✓ Lead Magnet Ideas
- ✓ Social Media Posts
- ✓ Press Releases
- ✓ Landing Pages
- ✓ Much More

Try for Free!

Scan the QR Code or visit dibbly.com/create

Next level tools to help you grow.

Whether you're an aspiring author or international bestseller, we've got the tools to help you publish faster, distribute wider and manage your business easier.

Learn more by going to **d2d.tips/dale** and read on to discover some of what sets D2D apart:

- ✓ **Automated end-matter**
- ✓ **New Release Notifications for readers**
- ✓ **Payment Splitting for contributors**
- ✓ **Scheduled price changes**
- ✓ **Smashwords store coupons**
- ✓ **Universal Book Links via Books2Read.com**

 **It's print-on-demand reimagined.**

Create a paperback on draft2digital.com from your existing ebook with just a few clicks, and **create a full, wrap-around book cover from your ebook cover**. It really is that easy!

 **THE indie bookstore.**

Massive annual sales, self-serve promotion tools, and the **industry's best royalty rates** of up to 80% list. Readers love discovering breakout indie authors at smashwords.com.

Win **awards** and get **reviews** for **your book**

25% off your first purchase

bookawardpro.com

INTRODUCTION: FROM ACCIDENTAL YOUTUBER TO AUTHOR SUCCESS STORY

Imagine connecting directly with your ideal readers, building a loyal audience, and selling more books without relying on a traditional publisher, expensive marketing, or luck. YouTube makes that possible—and I'm proof that you can start small, learn as you go, and grow into the creator you want to become.

Long before YouTube, I made goofy home videos for an audience of two—a friend and myself. Now, I create videos for over 120,000 subscribers worldwide and millions more viewers. My younger self wouldn't have understood what I do today, but I know he'd appreciate it. I'd spend weekends making and rewatching my dorky skits using my family's VHS camcorder. While my early budding career in video didn't include content about writing or publishing, I was still an aspiring author and saw that as my chief love.

I always enjoyed expressing myself beyond writing alone, and while reading and writing were my dominant passions, video scratched a different creative itch. Though I briefly revisited making videos in college—filming my rock band's performances—it was purely for personal enjoyment and local distribution. YouTube existed then, but I only saw it as a place for random, low-effort uploads. My perspective didn't change until early 2016, when after nearly two years of struggling to earn a living from writing, I achieved a breakout success with my book, *An Ultimate Home Workout Plan*. That unexpected success opened my eyes to how video could finally intersect powerfully with my author career, setting the stage for YouTube to become a critical turning point.

I was already active across social media, so when my book, *An Ultimate Home Workout Plan,* hit #1 on multiple Amazon Best Seller Lists worldwide, a fairly established YouTuber reached out to me for an interview. He saw how much success I had and was genuinely curious about how I got to that position so he could share it with his audience. My interview went great, leading to an invitation for another interview with a different YouTuber.

After I was done with both interviews, I found my email inbox and social media direct messages flooded with questions. I was more than happy to answer everyone, but the issue was that it took time away from what I loved doing most: writing and publishing books. After answering a few dozen emails, I realized that most questions were the same, so I needed to create a list of boilerplate answers that I could simply copy and paste. Since I was putting *that* much work into it, why not just record it? After all, I spoke faster than I typed, and I had some experience in video from my previous efforts.

Enter YouTube.

Back in 2016, YouTube was already huge, boasting around 1.4 billion monthly active users. I had no clue just how crucial this platform

INTRODUCTION: FROM ACCIDENTAL YOUTUBER TO AUTHOR SUCCESS STORY

would become for my author business, nor did I expect its growth to reach over 2.7 billion monthly users today.[i]

That April, I concluded YouTube was the perfect solution; it helped other authors without distracting me from my writing. Some of my peers shared how I didn't owe anyone answers, but that's not my nature. I saw myself in many of these authors reaching out and genuinely wanted to help.

Well, I launched a series of videos to the sound of crickets. Yep, my first videos—scratch that—my first year of videos yielded little to no results. It freed me up a bit, but the problem was that I now had even more people asking questions and needing my time. In June 2017, I finally committed myself to actually learning the craft of high-quality video content creation while exploring all that YouTube offered. Within a few months, my channel exploded to over 1,000 subscribers.

The best part about it was that I was already making a part-time income from consistent video publishing on YouTube, not to mention, I was selling a few more books (more about that in a future chapter) and earning additional revenue through affiliate marketing programs.

By the time early 2019 rolled around, I hit my next big milestone of 10,000 subscribers. I've often heard YouTube experts state that roughly 10% of YouTubers ever hit that level of success. You can imagine how excited I was, but there were always lingering questions in the back of my head: Was it all luck? Could I do it again?

So, I started a new channel specifically devoted to recording my audio podcast content. Reaching 10,000 subscribers on a second channel quickly resolved any remaining doubts or questions. Not to mention, I also was instrumental in the growth of another channel that nearly reached 10,000 subscribers (before I moved on to focus on my two established channels).

In 2022, I opened a secret YouTube channel that required little to no effort. And I mean it was real low effort, like less than ten minutes a week dedicated to recording and uploading content. I just used the same systems and best practices I picked up from years of being on YouTube, then applied them. By 2024, the secret YouTube channel qualified for the YouTube Partner Program, meaning that I could start making additional revenue from ads served on my videos.

As all my YouTube channels have grown, so have my book sales, reach, and influence. Having this massive platform affords me many opportunities I wouldn't otherwise have (i.e., interviews, sponsorships, conference invites, complimentary services, etc.). YouTube is so much more than a dumping ground for goofy home videos or sleazy online grifters. Like-minded people can meet, have fun, and get knowledge there.

While some folks would believe that I was born with some special gift for video content creation or had an established following, that couldn't be further from the truth. My YouTube success wasn't luck; it came from using proven systems and best practices consistently.

Since embracing YouTube, I've:

- Grown two channels to a combined 120,000 subscribers
- Successfully monetized four separate YouTube channels
- Boosted my author income and visibility by turning subscribers into loyal readers and book buyers

I've always been happy to share both my successes and failures. Rather than have you repeat the thousands of mistakes I made, I'll clearly highlight every pothole and pitfall so you can succeed faster than I ever did.

In the coming chapters, I'm going to walk you through everything from the fundamental understanding of YouTube to the more advanced strategies for fully monetizing your efforts while sacrificing as little author time as possible. YouTube shouldn't be just another shiny object for you to chase that brings no results, so you're going to be easing your way into it. Should the day come when you want to invest more time and effort into it, you can do that. For now, let's spare your writing and publishing time so you don't resent the process of video content creation.

I'll also remove most of the friction in deciding the type of content to publish on YouTube. Yes, what you produce and how often you produce it makes a tremendous difference in your platform's growth. You can stop banging your head against the wall, because you'll have a clearer understanding of the direction you should go that still honors your author brand.

For authors that are reluctant to get on camera or are afraid that their content doesn't measure up, I'll share precisely what invalidates any fear or reservation so that you can confidently produce your best content every time. No, you don't have to be on camera if you don't want to. That's the beauty of YouTube. But I'll show why your face is the best way to brand yourself and get wider recognition.

Much like the business of self-publishing books online, videos function in the same way with search engine optimization, keywords, and solid content. You'll see the secret to how I dominated the self-publishing niche for search terms for the past nine years on YouTube and Google. But I'll further share how there's one highly overlooked element to massive exposure through YouTube. (Hint: It has nothing to do with search traffic.)

Most important of all, you'll find out exactly how to build a loyal viewership and a community that knows, loves, and supports you. It's not enough that you publish videos and walk away from them. I'll show you some of my techniques for boosting video engagement and channel activity.

I don't expect everyone to have had the same experience as I had growing up. All you need is a desire to get more readers, sell more books, and diversify your author revenue. Even if there's a little spark in you right now, I can assure you it'll be a bonfire by the time you're done reading.

It's my hope you don't just consume the content but put it into action. Don't wait. Do it now. An imperfect action always trumps no action at all. You'll soon see why YouTube is one of the best platforms online today for authors. Delaying your journey will only hold you back from some incredible opportunities.

In the pages ahead, you'll learn exactly how to:

- Create engaging video content that naturally sells your books
- Attract and retain loyal subscribers who become dedicated readers
- Boost your discoverability and reach with simple yet powerful YouTube search engine optimization (SEO)
- Monetize your YouTube channel effectively, creating additional revenue beyond book royalties

Whether you're just getting started on YouTube or already have some experience, this book gives you practical strategies to grow your author brand, boost book sales, and confidently harness the full power of video. By the end, you'll know exactly how to use YouTube to build the author career you've always envisioned.

Let's dive in!

CHAPTER 1:
GETTING STARTED WITH YOUTUBE

When I officially launched my first YouTube channel dedicated to self-publishing, I didn't know what I was doing. I just knew that I had to show up in order to get any form of success. Sadly, my expectations were lofty compared to the reality. Sure, I had my share of viewers coming to watch my videos, but the results were modest, with videos getting anywhere from 3 to 100 views (if I was lucky). The few viewers that commented left positive feedback and provided recommendations for future videos.

Sliding into my second year of producing content, I questioned if YouTube was merely another time suck or if I could truly make something of this little side quest from my normal author adventure. It became rather defeating when I saw other video creators explode onto the scene and bring in hundreds of thousands of views and new subscribers within months, weeks, or even days.

I couldn't understand how others were doing well with just a few videos, while I had published dozens of videos for a focused audience of authors and self-publishers with little more than a few minor victories and an occasional compliment. I was too busy blaming the platform rather than focusing on what *I* was doing wrong.

I hadn't really become a student of the game, and the little success I got was from cobbling various bits of information shared by YouTube experts. However, the advice back then was rather nebulous:

- Publish videos consistently
- Niche down
- Use keywords for SEO
- Model your content off successful content creators

While that advice still holds true today, it's still not specific about what it is you could and should do based on the audience you want to serve. You shouldn't do what I did if you want to gain any momentum on YouTube for your author brand. I launched a channel about writing and self-publishing even though my published books were in the fitness niche.

Sure, a small subsection of my viewership might appreciate my fitness books. When viewers come to watch a channel about self-publishing, the best books to provide them would be about self-publishing. Yes, fitness books are great for everyone, but the people who showed up to watch my videos weren't there for lessons on push-ups and bodyweight squats. They were there to learn about self-publishing; that's it.

I didn't let the lack of results discourage me enough to quit, because I shifted my mind into learning mode and consumed as much information as I could about making it on YouTube. I'd watched countless hours of tutorials, webinars, and video courses.

In June 2017, I had a lightbulb moment. I saw parallels between publishing books and videos. The process is nearly identical if you break down the entire system from ideation to publication to promotion and beyond. With this newfound understanding, I implemented a daily video launch strategy based on Brian G. Johnson's *Tube Ritual*.

Tube Ritual's foundation is the belief that YouTube triumph stems from consistent effort, smart planning, and audience-focused videos, not random chance or viral sensations. Driven by my overachieving personality, I committed to daily uploads. I had more ideas than I had time and soon put my author business on simmer while I figured things out on YouTube.

In my first year, I gained over 500 subscribers, 19,000 views, and had over 1,059 watch time hours (the combined amount of time everyone viewed my content). By October 2017, I more than doubled my subscribers, views, and watch time. I learned over four months what content resonated the most with viewers, when the best time and day was to publish a video, and how to efficiently plan, shoot, and edit videos.

Thankfully, I got off the daily upload treadmill because it was overkill for my niche. The viewers weren't looking for daily advice and, more importantly, the 80/20 rule was at play here. About 20% of the content was bringing in 80% of the results. Sure, I didn't have a great batting average, but I was still successful in proving that YouTube isn't just luck or showing up.

To be clear, I don't recommend daily uploads unless you have the time and skill set. Those four months were tough, with twelve to sixteen hours a day spent creating videos while continuing to manage tasks for my self-publishing business. Thankfully, my fitness books were selling like hotcakes, and I already had a few titles queued up for release. That gave me the freedom to focus on YouTube while the publishing side of things kept moving with minimal effort.

How do you know if YouTube is right for you? Will this path require a ton of time, money, and extra resources? Can authors still find success launching a channel, even with so many creators already out there? Let's walk through what it takes to turn YouTube from a side hustle into a serious asset for your author business, including how monetization really works, why it matters, and what to expect as you build toward it.

NEW TO YOUTUBE? DON'T WORRY.

If some of the terms in this book feel unfamiliar—like YouTube Studio, thumbnails, or analytics—you're not alone. Many authors reading this are brand-new to video creation. You don't need to understand it all right away. I'll walk you through the more technical stuff step by step in later chapters, and you'll get the hang of it as you go.

In the meantime, consider watching a few beginner-friendly videos on YouTube (like "how to use YouTube Studio" or "YouTube for beginners"), or bookmark Chapter 8, which breaks things down in a hands-on way. You've got this.

WHAT IS THE YOUTUBE PARTNER PROGRAM AND WHY SHOULD AUTHORS CARE?

Many authors share concern over the ability to make money using YouTube. Most new video creators have probably heard about the YouTube Partner Program, the option to monetize your channel through ads served on or around your content. However, you do not need to be part of the YouTube Partner Program to make money on YouTube. Later, we'll discuss some ways authors can earn money right away without YouTube's intervention.

This shouldn't stop any author from looking into the YouTube Partner Program as a viable option to earn additional revenue. To qualify for the YouTube Partner Program, you must have:

- At least 500 subscribers
- 3 public videos have been uploaded in the last 90 days
- One of the following requirements is met:
  - 3,000 watch time hours of publicly available regular video viewing over the last 365 days
  - 3 million views of Shorts public videos in the last 90 days[ii]

With basic access to the program, you unlock these monetization tools:

- **Super Chat and Super Stickers**: Let viewers tip you during livestreams using interactive features that highlight their messages in real time.
- **Super Thanks**: Enables one-time tips on prerecorded videos, making support possible even when you're not live.
- **Channel Memberships**: Offer exclusive content, perks,

or behind-the-scenes access in exchange for a monthly contribution. This can create a steady, recurring income stream from your most engaged audience.
- **YouTube Shopping**: Sell books and merchandise directly through Shopify, Spring, or Spreadshirt. Once enabled, your channel gets a Store tab and a product carousel beneath your videos.

For anyone wanting a higher return, you'll want the more advanced access to the YouTube Partner Program. To qualify, you'll need:

- At least 1000 subscribers
- And one of the following requirements:

    o 4,000 watch time hours of publicly available regular videos watched in the last 365 days

    o 10 million views of public Shorts in the last 90 days

You get everything included in the basic access, plus ad revenue and YouTube Premium membership income. The first option will allow you to place ads on or around your video. The most prominent placements include the pre-roll, mid-roll, and post-roll ads where you can have an ad before, during, and after your video. Yes, the more ads you serve to your audience, the more revenue you'll make. Just don't go overboard with mid-roll ads, because some viewers will get fed up and just leave.

To be clear, you do not have to enable any of these monetization features in order to make money from YouTube. The Partner Program is merely an additional stream of revenue to reward you for your work. You won't face penalties for removing ads from your videos. This is a perfect segue into some common myths about YouTube.

BUSTING COMMON MYTHS ABOUT YOUTUBE FOR AUTHORS

One of the biggest misconceptions about YouTube is this unspoken philosophy of "if you build it, they will come." After all, you may have seen countless authors crushing it on the platform, so it's a given that any author can get the same results, right? Let's back up to when I mentioned how I identified parallels between the self-publishing business and YouTube. I should be a bit more specific: publishing on Amazon versus publishing on YouTube.

Both YouTube and Amazon distribute content through an algorithm-based platform where a sophisticated mathematical formula predicts the consumer's needs based on past behaviors. Just as millions of books compete for attention on Amazon, creators flood YouTube with every imaginable type of video, each one fighting for viewers' time and interest.

Amazon's algorithm favors products that consistently sell and YouTube rewards channels with longer watch time and a positive viewer experience. The reason YouTube likes watch time is so they can serve more ads to viewers through various placements on their site and in their videos. The revenue YouTube collects from ads then gets evenly divided between them and the video creator.

For the "if you build it, they will come" philosophy, you're banking on YouTube to serve your content to an eager audience. The reality is you'll need to create compelling enough content for viewers to want to tune in. Sadly, you won't truly know if they enjoy your video until you've launched it. Regardless of how much time, money, and effort you put into your content, it's a level playing field on YouTube for all videos.

Many authors believe that video content requires a large budget, fancy equipment, and high-priced video editing software. The reality is you don't need to be producing cinematic masterpieces. When my wife Kelli first broke onto YouTube back in 2018, she used the resources she had and never really upgraded. Her journey to getting fully monetized was ninety days.

Three months is all it took for my wife to crush it on YouTube. She used the webcam and onboard mic on her laptop and free editing software. To this day, Kelli keeps her YouTube business simple. She records her videos with her iPhone 11 and edits it with the free video editing software for Mac, iMovie.

In my first year, I failed to notice that viewers aren't always looking for fancy pants edits or over-the-top viral video tactics. They just wanted to get the information they needed so they could move on with their lives. Anything outside of their expectations was white noise.

This brings up another common myth: you need advanced tech skills. Nope! That's simply not true. Yes, when you break into video editing software for the first time, it'll be a bit overwhelming. Any time video editing was confusing, I simply searched for a solution on YouTube.

If you're still a bit too intimidated, you can go with a simple system for producing videos without the friction. It's dead simple:

1. Record the content
2. Upload the content

You might *think* basic videos with no editing would turn off viewers, but it can actually attract the type of viewers you want. The single largest video creator on YouTube is MrBeast right now, and he's built a massive platform from his viral videos. A team of world-class video editors meticulously produces every video. But it wasn't always that way. That channel started with screen recordings of video game play. He built his business up to that point from years of hard work, perseverance, and experimentation.

My friend Dan Currier had one video that completely changed the trajectory of his YouTube business. After a year of consistent weekly uploads, he had built an audience of about 500 subscribers. Then one video, filmed on his phone in his car during a lunch break, took off and pushed his channel into the thousands. By focusing on progress over perfection, he created something that resonated with viewers. That simple shift helped him gain thousands of new subscribers.

Sure, Dan is not MrBeast, but anyone could see the difference in content and the appeal for a mass audience. Where Dan helps video creators navigate YouTube, MrBeast produces story-based videos akin to short-form movies. They serve very different audiences, and that's the point—you don't need to be everything to everyone. Focus on the people your content is meant for and serve them well.

Another common myth is that YouTube favors longer videos. If that were true, I would've uploaded hour long videos from the start. But it's not just about length, you need to keep viewers engaged. Once someone starts watching, YouTube tracks how long they stick around. If they click away after a few seconds, the platform is less likely to recommend that content.

Let's address the biggest myth attached to video length:

CHAPTER 1: GETTING STARTED WITH YOUTUBE

All videos should be eight to ten minutes or longer.

This belief likely comes from YouTube's rules around mid-roll ads. A video must be at least eight minutes long to qualify, anything shorter won't allow mid-roll placement. While you can add as many mid-roll ads as you want, use common sense. Think like a viewer. Does placing an ad every 30 seconds make sense? Not really. Would one or two ads hurt a ten- to twenty-minute video? Probably not, but you'll need to test and see what works best for your audience.

The original requirement for mid-roll ads was ten minutes, hence why some video creators believe that's still the case.

Taking all that into account, you still do not have to monetize a video with ads. The team at YouTube has publicly stated many times that the algorithm doesn't favor monetized videos over non-monetized ones. The only concern is viewer satisfaction. If your viewers are happy, they'll stay longer and return for more later. You need viewers like that, so craft content that better suits their wants and needs.

One final myth needing a good busting is that you need to be on camera in order for this to work. While I believe creators who appear on screen are more likely to win over viewers, that doesn't mean everyone else is out of luck. Many faceless YouTube channels exist, proving you don't have to be the center of attention.

Are you lacking the desire to be on camera? That's okay, just record your voice. I wasn't comfortable when I first started and, even to this day, I still have issues. Since I tried, failed, learned from my mistakes, and never gave up, I slowly built an ability to be comfortable with a camera lens in my face.

Practice truly makes perfect, but it wasn't simply getting in the reps that helped me gain traction on YouTube. It had a lot to do with my singular focus and unwavering desire to make this work. That all comes from knowing what I want from YouTube and why I want it.

DEFINING YOUR GOALS & PURPOSE ON YOUTUBE

Before you ever break ground on YouTube, it's important to clarify why you're doing it and what you expect to gain. Jumping into video creation without a clear, defined path can lead to heartache and missed opportunities. That's why it's critical to identify your purpose and set specific targets. What you produce should reflect that purpose and move you forward. Every time you create a video that doesn't support that direction, you're wasting effort.

I encourage you to show up and stay consistent but do it with intention. For instance, since my channel is about self-publishing, would it make sense for me to publish videos about breeding albino goldfish? Probably not, since my target audience consists of authors. Even though I might see that the topic of breeding albino goldfish is huge, if it's not relevant to my purpose and goals, it's wasted movement.

Before you do anything else, get clear on why you're using YouTube in the first place. Are you trying to grow your platform so you can reach more readers? Or are you focused on building an additional stream of income to support your author career? There's no wrong answer—but knowing your reason will shape everything that follows.

My purpose for doing YouTube is to inform, educate, and update indie authors about all the relevant news and details in the world of self-publishing. I want YouTube to be an avenue where I can build more awareness of my author brand while generating additional revenue through the YouTube Partner Program, affiliate sales, and sponsorships.

Your reason doesn't have to match mine. Get clear on what you want from YouTube and why. When things get tough, having that clarity will remind you what matters most.

I once focused too heavily on content outside my audience's interests and paid the price. I'll break that down fully in Chapter 7, but let's just say it taught me a lot about staying true to your niche.

Once you establish your reason, it's time to set some goals. After all, how can you expect to get what you want if you don't have a clear and straight path that leads you to your desired outcome? I applaud the few video creators who can just wing it. For the vast majority of creators, planning is paramount.

Go through this list of questions to clarify your goals:

1. What specific audience do you want to reach with video? (Hint: It's not everyone.)
2. What type of content will showcase your niche, writing style, and brand effectively?
3. How often can you realistically upload videos to maintain consistency?
4. What is the core message you want to share in your videos?
5. How can you create videos that encourage positive viewer engagement?
6. What resources do you have for video production and editing? (More about that later.)

7. How will you measure success on YouTube? Be specific, whether that's a subscriber count or set monthly earnings.
8. How can you integrate your YouTube content with other marketing strategies?
9. What unique value can you offer that sets you apart from other authors on YouTube?
10. What's your one big, hairy goal on YouTube? Shoot for the moon!

Once you answer these questions, you should have a better understanding of the direction you want to take. Should you find you're stuck again, I highly recommend leaning on generative AI (artificial intelligence). While AI is still a divisive topic, I want to reassure everyone that I'm not insinuating you to abandon creative freedom.

All you need to do is answer those questions, share it with AI, then brainstorm the best goals for you on YouTube. The free version of most AI software should be sufficient. My preferred AI tools are Dibbly Create and ChatGPT. Sure, each tool has its limitations, but you're not trying to write an epic-length novel. You just need clear goals that outline your next steps on YouTube. For that, free access to AI should be more than enough.

CHAPTER 2:
PLANNING YOUR FIRST VIDEOS

The type of video content authors produce will determine how often they should post. I'd recommend starting with the path of least resistance: your genre.

Determine who your ideal reader is, and you'll most likely find them on YouTube in some capacity. With over 2.5 billion active users, you'll find your readers all over the platform. This is where you need to get good about what your ideal reader expects on YouTube, and not just your books.

Before planning any videos, define your ideal viewer. Yes, you're thinking about readers, but go deeper than that. What questions are they searching on YouTube? What problems are they looking to solve? What do they watch outside of your niche that still overlaps with your genre or brand?

This kind of research mindset works well for nonfiction authors, but fiction authors need to shift gears slightly. Instead of thinking like a teacher or guide, think like an entertainer or curator. Ask yourself: What kinds of stories do my readers love to get lost in? What tropes or genres make them click? Are they watching reviews, book hauls, dramatic readings, or character analyses? Fiction readers often come to YouTube to connect with stories, characters, and community. Your content doesn't have to solve a problem, it just needs to give them more of what they already love.

If you're not sure how to figure all this out, don't worry, we'll walk through how to study your niche on YouTube and find your audience before you ever hit record.

NOTE FOR BEGINNERS

If you're brand-new to YouTube and aren't familiar with terms like YouTube Studio, thumbnails, or analytics, don't worry. This book was written with beginners and intermediate creators in mind. I'll walk you through the more technical aspects when it matters most, and you don't need to absorb everything right away. YouTube Studio, for instance, is the dashboard where you manage your content and view important data like views and average watch time retention. It's available as a mobile app or through the desktop site (both work, though I personally prefer the desktop version for its full functionality). Just take your time and refer back to sections as needed. You'll get the hang of it.

Knowing your viewer's mindset, habits, and expectations gives your content direction razor-sharp focus. It helps you frame your videos, choose better titles, and speak their language. Don't assume you're just trying to find more readers; figure out who they are and what they care about most.

Even though thousands of authors are on YouTube, your voice still matters. The key is understanding what makes your content different.

Ask yourself:

- Are you educational, entertaining, motivational, or a mix of all three?
- Do you bring something to the table that others don't? (i.e., genre, experience, energy, or background)
- Are you the no-BS author, the kind coach, the behind-the-scenes builder, or something else entirely?

Positioning doesn't mean faking a persona; it means leaning into what already makes you unique. That's how viewers will remember you, recommend your content, and come back for more.

Just remember, authenticity only works if you bring energy and clarity to your delivery. If your videos are flat, full of filler words, or feel like you're second-guessing everything you say, most viewers will click away in seconds. Practice speaking with intention. Trim the rambling. And if you're not confident on camera yet, script your videos until you find your rhythm. You don't need to be over the top, but you do need to sound like you care.

It's okay if you're not sure yet. Just keep asking yourself:

> *Why would someone want to watch me instead of anyone else?*

Start by studying creators you already enjoy, especially those in your niche. What draws you to them? Is it their personality, their editing, their delivery, or their unique take on familiar topics? Take notes. Then turn that lens on yourself. Think about what makes you different as a writer, storyteller, or educator. Maybe you have a dry sense of humor, a calming presence, or a wildly creative brain that jumps between ideas. You don't need to reinvent the wheel; you just need to own what sets you apart and build from there.

DEFINE YOUR VERSION OF SUCCESS

Not every author needs 100,000 subscribers. For some, success means building an audience of 100 people who comment, engage, and buy every book they publish. For others, it's a platform to teach, speak, or build credibility in a niche.

The key is deciding early what success looks like to you. Is it book sales, email sign-ups, audience engagement, or goals like launching a speaking career, selling direct, or landing podcast interviews? There's no wrong answer, only one that aligns with your goals. When you're clear on your definition of success, it's easier to focus, avoid burnout, and stop comparing your growth to someone else.

Once you've defined your goals and started planning your content, it's easy to fall prey to perfectionism. Here are a few traps to watch out for before uploading your first video:

- **Waiting too long to start**: You don't need the perfect gear or channel branding to begin. You just need to hit record.
- **Chasing trends that don't fit your brand**: A viral video about trending book tropes might get views, but are they the *right* views?
- **Over-editing**: Fancy cuts and transitions aren't what make videos work. Viewers care more about your message.

- **Judging yourself too early**: Your first few videos are for learning, not perfection. Focus on progress over polish.

Every successful YouTube author once had zero subscribers and a shaky first upload. Your early videos are proof that you're serious, not flawless.

YouTube isn't just a platform to share videos; it can become the lifeblood of your author brand. Your content can funnel people into your mailing list, support book launches, and establish you as a trusted voice in your niche.

Ask yourself:

- Can I use this video to build anticipation for a book release?
- Should I mention my lead magnet or email newsletter in the description?
- Could this content live elsewhere too—like on Instagram, in a blog post, or as a Substack email?

Treat YouTube as an ecosystem engine, not so much a silo. Every video you make can do double or triple duty if you plan it with the rest of your author business in mind.

If I had the chance to start my YouTube journey over, I probably would have focused more on exercise videos. Each one could have included a simple call to action pointing viewers to my book. I would've shared the link in the video itself, in the description, and in a pinned comment (that's the top comment you choose to highlight on your video). That way, there would be no confusion about where to find the book I mentioned.

Okay, that's fine for nonfiction authors. What about fiction authors? You might instinctively think, "I'm going to produce videos about fiction writing, right?"

You could produce videos about fiction writing and I'm sure there'd be an audience of a few eager buyers. If you want to get more of your ideal reading audience, you need to be way more specific.

For my sci-fi horror brand, I could establish a channel that talks specifically to fans of that content. For example:

- Sci-fi horror book reviews
- Interviews with sci-fi horror authors
- Analysis of classic sci-fi horror novels and their impact on the genre
- Recommendations for undiscovered sci-fi horror literature
- Behind-the-scenes insights into writing sci-fi horror, including world-building and character development
- Live broadcasts of sci-fi read-alongs or storytelling sessions
- Discussions on the evolution of sci-fi horror and its cultural significance
- Video essays that explore silver screen adaptations of sci-fi horror books

If you write romance, you might create content like:

- Relationship tropes ranked or analyzed (e.g., enemies to lovers, fake dating)
- Booktube-style videos: "5 Romance Books That Made Me Cry"

- Short romantic stories or readings from your work
- "How I Write Kissing Scenes" or "My Top Romance Writing Tips"
- Behind-the-scenes of your outlining or character-building process
- Reaction videos to romantic movie scenes (and what they get right/wrong)

If you write fantasy, try these ideas:

- Deep dives into your worldbuilding: magic systems, lore, creatures
- Character breakdowns: "Meet My Dragon-Riding Heroine"
- Fantasy book reviews or tier lists (e.g., best fantasy villains)
- Timelapse videos of map sketching, cover reveals, or mood board creation
- Q&A sessions about your mythology or writing process
- Tropes in fantasy that you love or hate

The list could go on, but I'll wrap it up there since you might understand the point by now. However, if you're still stumped and unsure of the direction you want to go, then it's time for you to pay a visit to YouTube. Whether you're considering reviews, live readings, serialized fiction, or full audiobook uploads, you'll find examples of authors doing it successfully. And don't get hung up on subscriber count. I've seen small channels—some with under 1,000 subscribers—earn more than much larger ones simply because they connect deeply with their audience and offer the right products or services.

If you're still unsure what your readers are watching, try creating a separate YouTube account dedicated to your genre research. Use this profile only to watch content related to the niche you plan to publish in. Avoid anything outside that focus.

Visit YouTube and do a quick search for any keyword phrase associated with your niche. For me, that could be something simple like:

- Best sci-fi horror books
- Sci-fi horror story ideas
- Psychological sci-fi horror
- Sci-fi horror book recommendations

Complete the search and choose a video that best aligns with what resonates with you and your potential audience. Watch the video in its entirety, and if you like it, click the like button. Should the content be stellar, subscribe to the channel. Once that video is done, choose any of the recommended videos on the right side. Much like the first time, you'll want to select a video that interests you and your audience. Ignore anything outside of your niche, no matter how tempting it might seem.

Rinse and repeat this cycle as many times as you can afford time-wise. Once you're done, close out YouTube and come back to it in the next day or so. This time, when you visit YouTube's home page, you should get additional recommendations similar to the content that you watched and liked. Pick the video that seems the most appealing and watch.

Pay close attention to these elements:

- **Title and thumbnail:** These are the first things viewers see. The title tells them what to expect, while the thumbnail is the clickable image representing the video. It's like a book cover. If it doesn't grab attention, viewers will scroll right past it.

- **Style and pacing**: Pay attention to how the video looks and feels. Does it move quickly or take its time? What kind of energy does the creator bring? Are there long pauses, fast cuts, or steady talking points? These choices shape the viewer's experience.
- **Calls to action**: Watch how the creator encourages viewer interaction. Do they plug a product, mention their book, or ask for comments? Notice where and how they place these asks—early, mid, or end—and think about how their approach might work for you.
- **Viewer engagement**: Scroll through the comments. Look for more than just compliments. Are people asking questions? Offering criticism? Sharing their own stories? That kind of interaction gives you clues about what resonated and what didn't.
- **Recommended videos**: Check out the sidebar (or home feed if you're browsing later). YouTube suggests videos based on your watch history, so the more you engage with your niche, the better tailored your recommendations become. Bookmark any strong ideas you come across.

Once you have a clearer understanding of what's effective and what's falling flat on YouTube, it's time to roll up your sleeves and get to work. Let's put the tech aside for now and focus purely on pre-production for your video.

You might've heard that writers tend to fall into one of two camps:

1. Pantsers – also called discovery writers, they rely heavily on improvisation.
2. Plotters – these writers map out their work in advance to avoid unnecessary turbulence.

Yes, some writers have a little bit of both (yours truly being 60% plotter, 40% pantser).

Here's the fun parallel between authorship and video content creation: they're exactly the same. Some folks can turn on a camera with little more than an idea and make some stellar video content. While other video creators need to outline and even script the entire video.

What's the best way for authors to create video content? It depends. Just like with writing, you probably didn't figure out whether you were a pantser or plotter the moment you picked up a pen. You'll need to try creating videos before you uncover your own style. With time and practice, you'll figure out what works best for you.

I started out improvising all my videos, but the problem was the content was boring, sluggish, and often redundant. I knew generally what I was going to talk about, but I never really wrote anything down or planned it out. Unsurprisingly, those videos performed poorly.

When I finally started drafting a simple outline or a list of bullet points, the videos were much easier to improvise since I knew the direction I was going. The next issue I discovered was that I made a lot of mistakes doing improv and I simply didn't have the time or patience to keep editing my videos. That's when I decided to fully script my content.

Holy smokes! That cut down my editing time drastically. The very few mistakes I'd make were easy to clip, so I could focus on other aspects of my video content creation (i.e., thumbnail graphics, keywords, etc.). However, this required much more work upfront from me compared to the outlines or all-out improv sessions. The trade-off was worth it because I wasn't torturing myself with the battery of outtakes and additional time poured into editing the video.

At the very least, anyone new to YouTube should consider a basic outline before they shoot. Keep that outline close to the camera so it's easy for you to access it as you record.

SIMPLE VIDEO PLANNING TEMPLATE

Producing a video is like writing a book in that you'll have a piece that has the three-act structure: the beginning, middle, and end. If you're wanting to create videos with storytelling, this should come naturally. If you're producing straightforward informational videos like I've done, you'll want to follow the same structure but break it out in actionable chunks.

1. **Strong hook**: Start with a bold, curiosity-driven statement or question that grabs attention right away.
2. **Core content**: Get straight to the point. This is what your viewers expect, and it should make up the bulk of your video.
3. **Video handoff**: Avoid wrapping up with phrases like "in conclusion" or "final thoughts," since they often cause viewers to click away. Instead, end with a call to action that suggests another video on your channel. This keeps viewers engaged and signals to YouTube that your content deserves to be promoted.

Granted, this isn't a granular view of my video outlining process, but it at least gives you a jumping off point. Remember, as you're studying videos in your niche, you'll discover things that you and the viewers like and dislike about the content. Take notes, because you're getting the blueprint to success on YouTube based on what viewers currently know, like, and trust.

ESSENTIAL EQUIPMENT (WITHOUT BREAKING THE BANK)

Don't invest money you can't afford to lose. Start with what you already have. Take inventory of the tech and tools at your disposal:

- **Internet access**: This is the baseline for running anything online.
- **Camera**: Your phone, laptop, or desktop webcam is fine. Fancy gear won't guarantee views. Upgrade later as your channel grows.
- **Microphone**: Built-in mics work, but if you can, upgrade to a basic USB mic or lavalier. Many solid options cost between $15 and $100.
- **Lighting**: Viewers need to see you clearly. Start with sunlight and use lamps or overhead lighting if needed. If you're making faceless videos, this isn't essential.
- **Video editing software**: Free tools like DaVinci Resolve (desktop) or CapCut and iMovie (mobile) can get the job done. Expect a learning curve, but plenty of tutorials are out there.
- **Graphic design software**: Use Canva, GIMP, Photoshop, or something similar to create your thumbnails.

Optional tools to consider:

- **Screen capture software**: Needed for tutorials or faceless content involving your computer screen.
- **Digital masking technology**: Use avatars or animated characters to stay off camera while still showing "someone" on screen.
- **Livestreaming software**: OBS is powerful and free. For an easier setup, try Streamyard or Restream.

If you're working with a limited budget, what should you upgrade first? Start by evaluating what you already have. I always prioritize audio first, viewers need to hear you clearly. Video quality matters too, but it's secondary. Audiences will forgive a grainy image, but if they can't hear you, they won't stick around.

Around 2018, I collaborated on a video with my friend Julie Broad, founder of Book Launchers. We recorded in a shared hotel dining area with other guests nearby. When I went to edit the footage, I discovered I hadn't plugged in Julie's mic. Instead of scrapping the video, I boosted the audio from my mic whenever she spoke.

Bad idea.

Every time Julie spoke, the background noise drowned her out. Viewers let me know right away that they couldn't hear her. I learned two invaluable lessons:

1. Always check a mic before recording. Run a test and play it back.
2. Never publish videos with inferior quality sound.

Free video editing software is more than enough for most creators, so I don't see much reason to upgrade. If you want to invest in something, focus on your equipment (whether that's a new computer, laptop, or mobile device). Look for something that can handle video editing and has plenty of storage. You'll also want a system with ample memory and a modern graphics card to keep things running smoothly.

LOOK THE PART: YOUR ON-CAMERA PRESENCE

Getting your gear right is only half the battle. What your viewers see in the frame can make or break their trust in you, even if your message is gold. Before you hit record, take a minute to check the full picture:

- **Background & Environment:** Keep it clean, simple, and intentional. A cluttered room, messy bed, or pile of laundry behind you will quietly sabotage your credibility, even if your content is great. Find a neutral, tidy spot and make it your own. Good lighting helps, but a clean setup shows respect for your viewer's attention.
- **Foreground:** Don't crowd the space between you and the camera. Keep your desk or table clear of clutter unless it directly relates to your topic (like showing a book or mic setup). When you're on camera, *you* should be the focal point.
- **Clothing:** Dress for your brand and your audience. Viewers pick up on subtle signals. You don't need a suit or flashy outfit, but what you wear should reflect your message and not distract from it. A political tee while discussing fiction marketing? Probably not the right vibe.

- **Branding:** Subtle cues go a long way. A copy of your book on the shelf, a custom mug, or a channel logo in the corner of the frame. You don't need to go overboard but give people a reason to remember you.

You don't need a Hollywood set. You just need a space that looks put together, reflects your brand, and keeps attention where it belongs—on your message.

CREATING A COMFORTABLE FILMING SPACE

One of the biggest factors in my success, and in streamlining my workflow, was having a recording space I actually enjoyed being in. There's nothing worse than already dreading video creation, then having to do it in a space that doesn't show you at your best. I used to record in my living room, but that meant setting up and tearing down equipment every single time.

Once I knew I needed a separate office space, I ran into another issue: sharing that office space with my wife. Again, I faced the hassle of set up and takedown. What I really needed was a solid set that didn't require any extra work. That way, I could record a video on the spot. When I was setting up and taking things down, it created more friction and, therefore, created more reluctance to do the damned thing.

When I finally settled on the right area, I decorated the background with small LED lights and trinkets that I felt best embodied who I was as an author and video creator. These days I have two sets of bookshelves with LED lights and various Dale-related paraphernalia.

Since I also work in this space when I'm not shooting, it's extra special so that I always feel comfortable.

Do *you* need a separate office space or house? That's entirely up to you, but again, I recommend working with what you have. If you need to set up and take down a set every time you record, I recommend taking a picture of it and placing small markers where you have everything (i.e., light placement, chair, etc.).

Whatever you choose to use as your set is entirely up to you, so take your time. You might find it'll take awhile before you finally settle on something that works for you. If you start feeling excited about shooting videos, you're on the right track. It's even better if your recording setup can also serve as your writing area. I know I love it that way.

YOUR FIRST UPLOAD (WHAT TO EXPECT)

Your first uploads will feel nerve-wracking, but over time, the process gets less stressful. As long as you pay attention to your analytics and viewer comments, you'll keep learning and improving. For your first upload, focus on one thing: successfully shooting, uploading, and publishing your video.

Whether you get 5 views or 50,000 views, it's still a victory. I find videos are like books in that your first book is always going to be the most challenging. How could anyone prepare you for this business? The best action isn't in preparation, but in doing.

A few metrics you should pay closest attention to include:

　1. **Views:** Tracks how many times your video has been watched.

2. **Watch time retention:** Shows how long viewers stay engaged and where they drop off. You'll need to access YouTube Studio to see this data. It typically takes 24–72 hours for YouTube to process and display accurate retention stats. Keep in mind that if your video has very few views, those stats might be skewed and not reflect normal viewer behavior.
3. **Comments:** Reveals what your viewers are saying and helps you keep the conversation going. Later, we'll cover how this engagement can grow your YouTube community.

Are there other metrics for you to consider? Sure, but if it's your first video, you need little more than that. No one expects you to understand a new language just by studying for a day or two. Learn the language as you go and adjust accordingly.

Realistically, some of you are going to publish a video that gets no views. That's okay! I've published some duds before. I take a step back, figure out where I went wrong, then troubleshoot the best steps forward. You can do it too! Just don't lose heart when a video doesn't perform according to your expectations. That doesn't reflect your value as a person, it just means you have some learning ahead of you.

Whatever you do, avoid comparing yourself to other video creators. Sure, some channels blow up overnight with a single video, but they're the exception, not the rule. Focus on your own progress, and let your past work be the only benchmark you measure against. The more you grow on your terms, the more sustainable and rewarding the journey will be.

CHAPTER 3:
CREATING VIDEOS THAT KEEP PEOPLE WATCHING

C reating video content is simple to start. I wouldn't have even bothered with YouTube in 2016 if it was impossible. Anyone with a smart phone and a few thoughts can shoot a video, edit the content, then publish it. Video creators who make a real impact focus on crafting every video with intention instead of hoping their footage turns out well.

In the beginning, I recorded my videos using a low-quality laptop webcam and built-in mic. But the gear wasn't the only issue. Those early videos were visually rough, slow-paced, and lacked energy. Yes, the information was there, but viewers don't want to sit through a dull presentation just to find a few useful tips. They expect value up front. If they don't get it quickly, they'll move on.

Little by little, I refined my video production. The first things I changed include:

1. **Don't film when you're tired or uninterested.** Viewers can tell when you're not fully present or passionate about the topic.

2. **Keep your camera at eye level or higher.** Shooting from below looks awkward and unflattering. It also gives the impression you're looming over your audience.
3. **Maintain a comfortable distance from the camera.** You should be close enough for viewers to clearly see your facial expressions, but not so close that your face dominates the frame or feels intrusive. A medium shot—from about the chest up—usually works best.
4. **Use the rule of thirds.** Frame yourself in the center vertical third, and leave a couple of inches of space above your head for balance.

But these are just a few examples of what I learned early on, so let's dive deeper into crafting videos that hook your audience and keep them coming back for more.

WHAT VIEWERS ACTUALLY WANT FROM AUTHOR VIDEOS

Viewers are hoping to be educated, entertained, or inspired, and while you don't have to embody all three within a video, it can certainly go a long way by attracting a wider audience. When you're drafting ideas, you need to fulfill any of those three expectations easily.

For my videos, I've learned that education comes first with entertainment sprinkled in. That entertainment part is whenever I allow my goofy sense of humor to fly when it's appropriate to the video. That's not to say I haven't created videos that inspire authors (see my Book Rescue series), but I've found that educational videos with some entertainment are what my audience appreciates and expects.

You'll need to experiment with different types of content. Let the results guide your direction. But no matter what, stay true to yourself. Too many creators waste time trying to imitate others, and it gets them nowhere.

My earliest content showed me trying to be someone I wasn't. Sure, within a year, I started making them more entertaining, fast-paced, and insightful. But I still wasn't being fully authentic; I was trying to be who I thought my viewers wanted instead.

The sooner you can be okay with yourself in a video, the better, because your ideal viewers will come flocking to you. Does that confidence come overnight? No, but if you're consistent about producing and publishing videos while analyzing the results, you'll get better.

YouTube Studio gives you unfiltered data on how your videos perform. It's different from the main YouTube viewing platform. While YouTube is where people watch videos, YouTube Studio is where you manage your channel. To access it, go to the YouTube homepage, click your profile picture in the top right corner, then select *YouTube Studio* from the dropdown. Or go directly to studio.youtube.com if you're already logged in.

Here's what I monitor most:

1. **Views**: How many people watched your video.
2. **Watch time**: How long they watched, on average.
3. **Audience retention**: Under the *Overview* tab, check the graph to see where viewers stay or drop off.
4. **Average view duration**: Found in the *Engagement* tab. Higher is better.

5. **Click-through rate**: Under *Reach*, this shows how many people clicked your video after seeing the title and thumbnail. I aim for 5% to 10%, but results will vary.
6. **Comments**: These are valuable. They show what's working, what's not, and how your audience feels. Be open, but don't take every comment to heart.

YouTube Studio offers a robust set of tools for creators to explore. I recommend checking in weekly to track the results of your efforts. Two great channels to follow in this space are Creator Insider and YouTube Insider. Both share insights directly from the source to help you understand how the platform really works. You won't master this dashboard overnight. It takes time, patience, and ongoing research.

How a video performs has everything to do with what resonates the most with viewers. Many failed video creators will often blame the algorithm for their lack of success, and it really couldn't be further from the truth. YouTube built a sophisticated system of mathematical formulas based on audience satisfaction. If your video isn't performing well, it's not the fault of the algorithm. Either the video didn't meet audience expectations, or the content simply wasn't worthy enough to reach a larger audience.

Video creators need to be willing to take a step back, analyze where they went wrong, and adjust their approach. It's not fun to realize you put a ton of work into a video that underperforms. But you can learn a lot from every misstep or setback. Give yourself a little grace, learn from what's working, then purge what doesn't. Content creation is an iterative process if you're willing to put in the work, take your time to do the research, and ask vital questions about how you can make better videos.

STRUCTURING VIDEOS FOR MAXIMUM WATCH TIME

Capturing a viewer is one task that requires a solid title and thumbnail to entice viewers to watch. Once you've cleared that hurdle, it's up to the video content to keep viewers engaged and watching till the end. So, how do you structure the video to get the most watch time?

Shooting long videos will not get you anywhere if you're not keeping viewers for longer than a few seconds. Every video you publish needs to be clipped and edited in a way that focuses on audience satisfaction.

The most important part of your video will come within the first 15 to 30 seconds. You only have one chance to give viewers a compelling reason to watch, so you have to make it count. This means you shouldn't lead with a fancy, short animated bumper or rattle off who you are and what you do. The first words out of your mouth need to tell viewers exactly what to expect.

Since you have less than half a minute to hook viewers, you shouldn't waste a single word. I highly recommend drafting an opening hook, even if you plan to improvise your content. If you're not sure what you're going to talk about in the video, shoot the core content first, then record your hook.

As an example, my videos used to be structured like this:

1. Tell people what we're talking about in the video.
2. Roll a 15-second channel bumper I had made on Fiverr.
3. Tell people who I am, what I'm about, and to subscribe.
4. Ask viewers for a comment about the video's topic.
5. Insert the core content.
6. Summarize the content at the end before signing off.

Paying attention to my video analytics, I soon discovered viewers were dropping off massively at the beginning but continuing right when I was getting to the core content. In response, I shortened my channel bumper until it was three seconds long, but even then, I saw an enormous drop in viewers in the first minute.

I then removed the channel bumper altogether and discovered that more viewers were sticking around, but I was still seeing a large drop in viewers. My next task was to dial in my hook so that I could say it in less than two to three sentences. For example:

VIDEO HOOK (OLD WAY)

Today, I want to talk about how self-publishing is one of the best businesses for authors to consider and how easy it is, now more than ever.

VIDEO HOOK (NEW WAY)

Here are ten solid reasons self-publishing is perfect for new authors.

The first way isn't bad, but it goes on a little too long. For my video intros, I pretend I'm trying to share a tidbit with someone that's getting into an elevator. I want to articulate what I have to offer before that elevator door closes. The goal is to get that person to step off the elevator and hear me out. Avoid speaking too fast, because then they can't really hear or understand you. But you don't want to go too slow since the elevator door is going to close any second.

Once you get past that hook and you've got their attention, you can do one of two things:

1. Provide context with whom you are. Keep it short and to the point, much like the hook.
2. Go right into the core of your content.

The first way allows you to share who you are and what you do, just don't let it drag on with too many calls to action. I used to lean heavily on providing context until I tried something completely different with my script.

Even though I'd removed the channel bumper and tightened my hook, I was still seeing a drop off. I removed the contextual introduction and just got into my stuff. My thought was people can take a pretty strong guess about who I am and what I do based on what I'm talking about. The gamble paid off because I saw fewer viewers dropping off and longer watch time retention across all new videos.

You'll need to experiment to see what works best for you. I don't want to discourage you from bumpers or lengthy self-introductions, because it might be how you prefer to express yourself. However, if you find you're having a steep drop off at the beginning of your videos, it's time to reconsider your approach.

Once you have your viewers hooked, get to work. Don't spend too long dwelling on any one point or trail too far from what you promised in the hook. That's your North Star, your thesis, if you will. If you deviate from that path, either clip it or reshoot it. Your primary goal is to keep viewers watching, so remove as much of the friction as you can.

To be clear, there will be times when you go off track or just aren't feeling it. That's okay. Give yourself some grace. Even after nine years on YouTube, I still struggle with staying focused. The key is to learn from each misstep and apply those lessons to your next video.

Another area where authors often fall short on YouTube is promoting their books, products, or services. Yes, you should absolutely share with your viewers what you do and what you're all about. The trick is to organically weave a call to action in each video without derailing the flow.

For example, if I produced a video about Kindle Direct Publishing (KDP):

> **BAD:** *Hey, guys, my latest book,* Wide Publishing for Authors, *is out! I'm so proud of it and would really appreciate if you read and reviewed it. Go grab a copy everywhere today!*

> **GOOD:** *What if you're not really into Kindle Direct Publishing? Is there an alternative? I talk all about it in my two-time award-winning book* Wide Publishing for Authors. *Grab your copy at every major online retailer today when you visit DaleLinks.com/WideBook.*

The bad way was fine, but it feels slightly out of place in the middle of a video about KDP. Also, it's self-serving and focused entirely on how it benefits me and not the viewer.

In the better approach, I start with a strong hook and give viewers a clear reason to check it out right away. Then I tell them exactly where to find it. Saying it's available "everywhere" or "on Amazon" isn't specific enough. You need to remove any friction and give them the simplest path to take action.

You get bonus points if you include that link in your description, the video, and a pinned comment.

You'll find better and easier ways to provide a call to action for your books, products or services as you experiment with new formats and structures for your videos. A little time and testing will help you uncover the best ways to push your author business, but don't expect instant results or perfection right away.

As you're coming to the end of your video, keep it simple. Don't offer any summaries, goodbyes or any finalizing words like "finally" or "thanks for watching my video." You're indirectly telling viewers you're done with them and that they can move on. Don't allow them that opportunity. Instead, once you've wrapped your core content, send people to another video.

Within your YouTube Studio dashboard, you can add an end screen, where it includes a clickable channel subscription button, plus any videos you want to showcase. You have upwards of twenty seconds of the last video to place an end screen. I've found that using all twenty seconds is excessive since some viewers can sense a video is over once clickable elements populate their screens. Don't waste a single syllable on unnecessary words. Much like your hook, you need to create closing dialogue that guides viewers to another video.

The end screen is one of your best opportunities to guide viewers to take action, whether that's subscribing to your channel or checking out one of your books. But don't just drop a link or ask for a favor.

Give them a reason to care. If you mention a milestone, connect it to the value you offer. Instead of saying, "Help me reach 100,000 subscribers," explain what they'll get by sticking around. When your content clearly serves the viewer, subscribing or clicking through feels like the obvious next step.

FILMING WITH ENERGY AND CLARITY

Building confidence on camera takes time. Some people are naturals, but most of us need patience and plenty of practice. Across two channels, I've published over 1,700 videos, and I'm still working to improve my on-screen presence.

Again, I don't suggest that anyone publish over 1,700 videos overnight. That's over nine years of work. What will improve your on-camera presence is creating one video at a time.

The two most important areas you can focus on are energy and clarity in your delivery. Energy means showing genuine interest in your topic and speaking like you care about what you're saying. Viewers can tell when you're invested. While passion can grab attention, it won't hold it if your message isn't clear.

Communicating with clarity takes practice and also requires a lot of self-reflection and self-awareness. One way to tell if you're not being clear enough is through the comments. Viewers will ask questions you thought you already answered, or they'll say they're confused and need more direction. Fortunately, you never have to ask your viewers to leave feedback; they'll do it without prompting.

Take all criticism with a grain of salt, and try not to take it personally. If you're anything like me and not a professionally trained broadcaster or speaker, give yourself some grace. Even the best pros need practice and growth. No one is perfect, no matter the field.

A few tricks I do to speak naturally include:

1. **Speak slowly and deliberately** to give your audience time to process what you're saying.
2. **Pause often** to gather your thoughts and maintain a comfortable pace.
3. **Be okay with making mistakes**; perfection isn't necessary to be effective.
4. **Sit or stand with good posture.** It opens up your lungs for better breathing and signals confidence to both you and your viewers.

I have no problem speaking slower than usual and enunciating every word. Pausing and gathering my thoughts can be a challenge, but it helps prevent filler words or redundant speech. The latter of the tips is a bit more difficult, because when you're wanting to shoot a good video, sometimes mistakes will happen. Early on for me, a mistake would completely derail my thoughts and eventually, I'd lose my cool.

In 2017, I attended the video creator conference, VidSummit, to rub shoulders and learn from the greats on YouTube. Hundreds of people gathered for this conference and cameras were rolling everywhere. Some people walked and vlogged, while others conducted interviews in various corners of the event center. Between speaker sessions, I noticed my two friends, Nick Nimmin and Brian G. Johnson, shooting a video collaboration, so I pulled up a chair and just watched them do their work.

Every time Brian stumbled, he paused, lowered his head, took a deep breath, and then picked up right where he left off. On a few occasions, he had to reset two or three times before getting it right. When I asked him about his process, he turned the question around and asked how I made my videos. I explained that I usually script my content, so if I mess up a line, I have to back up the teleprompter, reset my mindset, and try again. With each take, my frustration would build until I felt like throwing my camera out the window.

Brian chuckled, then explained that it was unfair to expect to nail every shot perfectly. He further pressed that by getting mad it would only make the work harder. Thinking about it, I realized right then that the best videos I produced were ones where I hit a good flow and ignored the minor imperfections. Yes, you will make mistakes and a few of you might even have bad takes that are worth a laugh or two. The bottom line: don't let perfection stop you from producing content. Embrace the perfection in imperfection and you'll go far!

UPGRADING VIEWER EXPERIENCE (WITHOUT BIG BUDGETS)

Leveling up your video quality doesn't require expensive gear or the fanciest premium software. Sometimes, it's as simple as making the most of what you already have. A few minor adjustments can dramatically improve your final product.

For example, even a low-quality camera can deliver solid results with good lighting. Many budget models struggle in dim conditions, which leads to grainy or pixelated footage. A few well-placed lights can make a huge difference. I typically use two to three. Position your brightest one just in front of your left or right shoulder, keeping it out of frame to avoid overexposure. Use a softer light on the opposite side to create balance. If possible, add a third behind you, and let your body partially block or diffuse it. That backlight adds separation between you and the background. Use daylight bulbs wherever possible. They're bright, clear, and designed to make any room feel more professional on camera. Just be sure to use the highest wattage your setup allows, without overloading your gear.

It's not mandatory to have all those lights, but it can certainly go a long way. If all you have are a few windows and a couple lamps, then work with them. Avoid having a window directly behind you. Depending on the time of day, the sun could wash out your video, making it unwatchable.

To be clear, you will not find the perfect light placement right away. Experiment with brightness settings and placement. The clearer you can be on screen, the better.

Another way to boost your video quality is through better editing. Here's my basic process:

1. **Start with a double clap.** This creates a visible spike in the audio timeline, so I know where each new section begins.
2. **Import the footage** into your editing software.
3. **Segment the video** using the clap spikes to jump between sections.
4. **Make a rough cut.** Watch the full video and trim out filler, stumbles, or unnecessary words.
5. **Add visuals.** Use simple editing elements like text labels on screen (called lower thirds), basic scene changes (transitions), and extra footage (b-roll) to keep your video visually interesting. If there's a hard cut mid-sentence, I'll either

zoom in slightly to create a smooth shift or drop in a cut-away clip as a buffer.
6. **Review from start to finish.** Treat this like proofreading a manuscript. Fix anything rough and re-record segments if needed.
7. **Render and publish.** Once everything looks good, export your video and get it out into the world.

Though this process is basic, it can be time-consuming, so you don't have to follow my blueprint exactly. Take parts in each process and adopt them as your own. Ultimately, you'll want to shoot the video, edit it, then publish it. That's it.

Don't go overboard clipping and trimming your video because it becomes distracting if you do it too much. It's okay to let your monologue flow freely.

Between 2016 and 2020, retention editing was the buzzword for video creators. Popular YouTubers made it their mission to keep viewers watching from beginning to end without ever having the temptation to leave. The practice involves using techniques such as strategic pacing, engaging visuals, compelling storytelling, and effective use of hooks at the beginning of the video (see earlier advice). The goal is to reduce viewer drop-off and maximize viewer retention, which positively impacts the video's performance on YouTube.

The problem is that retention editing became a parody of itself, with some creators clipping, splicing, and overlaying footage with tons of visual effects for the sake of it. I subscribed to this system and believed it's what I needed to hit the big time.

It wasn't. My viewers wasted no time letting me know what they didn't like about my approach to retention editing:

1. "Stop zooming in and out. Just keep the camera still."
2. "That background music is distracting. Get rid of it."
3. "Enough with the sound effects, we're not three years old."

I've forgotten dozens more similar complaints. It bruised my ego a bit, but I swallowed my pride and began making the changes. Lo and behold, my videos performed better, and people watched for longer.

A small trick that makes a big impact is the pattern interrupt. Let's say you've been filming a monologue from your office chair. In the next shot, try switching locations or pick up the camera and talk while walking. This simple change breaks the usual flow and gives viewers a fresh visual. Disrupting the pattern helps reset their attention and keeps them engaged in your content.

Don't go too crazy on pattern interrupts because you don't want your videos to become annoying. The comments can range from "Stop moving from one room to the next, Dale! Geez!" or "Okay, why do you keep appearing in one room then the next. Just hold still!"

You'll know your video is ready when it feels right. I know that sounds vague, but it's true. Only you can decide when a video feels finished. Lead with your best effort, don't chase perfection, and pull the trigger. If you're feeling unsure, ask another video creator to review it. Sometimes, I'll share an unlisted YouTube link with members of my Discord community and invite their honest feedback.

It's incredibly helpful to have someone else watch and review your videos. They'll catch small issues like typos on screen or missed outtakes. Just like with books, a second set of eyes can strengthen the content before it goes live. Videos tend to look more polished when more than one person is involved in the review process.

> *Quick tip: Upload your video to YouTube Studio and save it as Unlisted. Share that link with only the people you trust. When you're ready to publish the video, simply put the video to Public or Schedule it, then hit save.*

Once the video is available to the public, I'll monitor its performance closely for the first twenty-four hours, then lightly check up on it daily for the next week. Remember that even though a video might not do well upon launch doesn't mean it's doomed to obscurity and is a complete failure. Some videos can take off months down the road. If you ever want to see a video perform better, test out new titles or thumbnails.

THE TRUTH ABOUT VIDEO LENGTH AND RETENTION

How long do you make your books? I'm hoping you're confidently answering that you make your book as long as it needs to be for your genre, and you craft every sentence like a seasoned artisan. Your videos are similar in that regard.

However, if you're brand new to video, start with five to ten minutes of content. Keep in mind, there is a lot of work in planning, prepping, shooting, and editing videos. Shorter videos mean shorter production time. You need quick victories, so don't bog yourself down by creating an epic-length masterpiece for your first video.

Popular YouTube Expert Roberto Blake often shares that you should publish 100 crappy videos. He's not implying that you forever churn out trash content. The thought is you keep publishing and improving upon your content with each new release. Once you hit 100 videos, you'll see a remarkable difference in video quality.

Your primary goal on YouTube is audience retention. Yes, longer videos can be good, but if the viewers aren't watching it for very long, YouTube is less apt to suggest your content to other viewers. Once you keep that audience watching for longer periods of time, then you'll get more recommended and search traffic from YouTube. Just remember to produce the best video you can. Length will come in due time with practice and patience.

CRAFTING CTAS THAT DON'T FEEL PUSHY

Have you seen video creators who ask viewers to like, subscribe, comment, and share? The call-to-action (CTA) is for viewers to help gain favor from the YouTube algorithm. There's some truth to that, but could you spend that time more wisely or with sharper focus? Absolutely.

The first thing you need to do is get good at what your video accomplishes. Do you want more subscribers? Great! Do you want to promote your latest werebear shapeshifter romance novel? Fantastic. Decide before you shoot a video on what you want to accomplish and stick to that mission.

Can you deviate and create another CTA outside of what your video offers? Sure, but put yourself in the seat of someone who doesn't know you. The vast majority of viewers who watch your content won't know you. Treat it as such. Would you ask for four or five favors from a complete stranger? Probably not, so stick to that one good CTA.

This means choose what you're encouraging. Do you want more likes? Then ask for it. Do you want comments? That's easy, just ask for your audience's opinions. Make the question compelling enough for someone to want to chime in. Would you like your content shared? Then, make that video rock solid, then ask viewers, "If you enjoyed this video, could you share it with someone else who'd enjoy it too?"

I prefer to put my calls-to-action around the middle to end of my videos because that gives me plenty of time to deliver value. Once I've met a viewer's expectations, they are then more likely to act based on what I requested. The CTA I most often use is the end screen hand-off. Once I'm in the last ten to twenty seconds, I'm cuing up viewers with another video that perfectly relates to the current video's theme.

For selling books, get to the point. We know you love your book, but you've got only seconds to shift a viewer's mindset. Because once you go from delivering value to asking for viewers to buy your book, your audience is starting to either:

1. Skip forward in the video.
2. Leave the video altogether.

The first option isn't bad because at least they're sticking around to watch the rest of your video. The latter option isn't good at all because you lost a viewer, therefore your overall watch time drops. How do you avoid losing viewers while advertising your book? Creativity!

You're an author; think of creative ways to interject your book into the conversation. You can ease into it like:

> *"Now that I've shown you the ten best places to publish your books, check out even more options in my two-time award-winning book* Wide Publishing for Authors, *available at every major retailer and library when you visit* DaleLinks.com/WideBook.*"*

The previous example shows what I'd say at the end of a top ten list, so I would've demonstrated value by then. The next logical conclusion is that the viewer can learn more in my latest book, so they grab a copy.

Fiction authors can approach their content the same way, weaving their books naturally into the themes, emotions, or topics they already explore in their videos.

For example, if you're reviewing dystopian novels or breaking down tropes in dark fantasy, you might say:

> *"If you're into stories like this, you'll probably enjoy my novel* Ashes of Tomorrow. *It leans into similar themes of survival and rebellion. You can find it on Amazon or check the link below."*

The goal isn't to interrupt the flow, it's to build momentum toward your book. If the content aligns with your story's themes, world, or tone, then the mention feels earned. You're not forcing your book into the conversation—you're showing how it belongs there. Over time, this gentle, consistent reinforcement builds familiarity and trust, which makes potential readers far more likely to buy.

You don't need to pitch your book in every single video. However, you should always include *some* kind of call to action. That could be asking a question, suggesting another video, or sharing a link to your email list. Mentioning your book should feel like a natural extension of the topic, not a sales gimmick. If every video ends with "Buy my book!" you'll lose viewers. But if each video gently moves people deeper into your world, your books, or your mission, you'll build a loyal following that sticks around and eventually buys.

Be consistent with your calls-to-action and you'll see rewards in the long run. I've had plenty of revenue come in from old videos I published years ago. This works best with evergreen content, but even time-sensitive videos can still bring value over time. Don't feel discouraged if you don't see the results that you want right away. I would recommend you test one CTA for a handful of videos before you determine the effectiveness. If you're not seeing sales, likes, or subscribers, change up your strategy. As long as you're producing content with the viewer in mind, whatever call-to-action you use is incidental. Make it less disruptive and more of a welcomed change.

One of my favorite content creators is Ten Hundred, an art YouTuber who seamlessly integrates sponsored ads so well that I don't just want to watch the commercial, I feel like I have to. As he talks about his sponsors, I'm fixated on time-lapse of his artwork or behind-the-scenes footage that is relevant beyond the commercial.

Think of a creative way you can do the same. How can you get viewers to continue watching while also feeling invested in your CTA? This is where you can get creative. It might not come right away, but it'll come with some experimentation. Good luck!

CHAPTER 4:
GETTING DISCOVERED - YOUTUBE SEO THAT ACTUALLY WORKS

UNDERSTANDING HOW YOUTUBE SEARCH WORKS

When you search engine optimize (SEO) your video, you're using specific keywords that have high demand among viewers. In theory, by placing these high demand keywords strategically in your title, description, tags, and video dialogue, you're making your video more discoverable.

However, that's only part of what YouTube uses to serve your video to a wider audience. Some experts have even stated that tags are nearly worthless and that descriptions play a factor in search, but it's all predicated on viewer satisfaction. If viewers aren't happy with a video, they're less apt to serve it to a wider audience.

> *Side note: Tags are still in the YouTube backend, but they're no longer a major <u>factor in discovery</u>. If you use them, stick to five to ten broad but relevant terms as a fallback. Hashtags can be helpful if you're organizing a series or theme, but they won't drive much traffic on <u>their own</u>.*

For new video content creators, leveraging search-based discovery will yield the quickest results, so lean into keyword-rich titles and watch for trends within your niche. The easiest way to find those keywords and patterns is by spending time on YouTube. Earlier, I suggested opening a separate YouTube account to study videos in your niche. By now, you've probably started spotting recurring words and phrases in titles and descriptions. These patterns show you what viewers actually search for, and you can use them to guide your content.

YouTube is owned by Google, so its search algorithm works similarly to how Google ranks content. That means your videos can appear in both YouTube and Google search results, making keyword research even more valuable.

Use common keywords but make the content your own. It's fine to draw inspiration from others, but don't outright copy someone else's video idea. Mimicking someone else will only hold you back. You have something unique to offer, so let it show. Get creative with your title choices and lean into your own voice.

I organically weave keywords within every description with one simple tool: AI. Artificial Intelligence is great for a variety of tasks in business, including:

1. Providing relevant keywords
2. Brainstorming titles
3. Drafting a description
4. Building a list of tags

STEP-BY-STEP PROMPT FOR AI METADATA CREATION

For this, I use either Dibbly Create's ChatKIP or ChatGPT. Create a dedicated conversation thread for this work so you can easily track everything in one place. The best way to cue up AI is to provide the script, outline, transcript, or brief description of the content. For instance:

> I'm creating a YouTube video designed to help (target audience, e.g. self-published authors, fiction writers, readers of X genre, etc.). I need a full metadata package to optimize the video and increase watch time and engagement.
>
> **MY VIDEO TOPIC:**
>
> (Insert your video idea. Be as specific as possible.)
>
> **MY GOALS:**
>
> - (Example: educate, entertain, drive book sales, grow community, promote a tool, etc.)
>
> **KEY POINTS THE VIDEO WILL COVER:**
>
> - (List 3–5 things your video will talk about.)
>
> **I NEED THE FOLLOWING DELIVERABLES:**
>
> - A YouTube video title (under 60 characters) that is curiosity-driven and avoids spoilers. It should create urgency, be easy to read at a glance, and appeal to my niche audience.

- A video description (3–4 sentences) that teases what viewers will learn or discover without giving everything away. Include any affiliate links, calls to action, or follow-up content if needed.

- A video tag paragraph (SEO keywords, separated by commas, under 500 total characters) optimized for search, discoverability, and relevance.

- Thumbnail text variations that don't repeat the video title but add intrigue or amplify the hook.

Whenever you find the output to be unsatisfactory, request AI to ask questions to clarify any ambiguities or unclear areas. If you don't lead AI in the right direction, it'll most likely give you subpar results. Think of it like a genie in the lamp. You can get your wishes granted, but you had better word it right or face the consequences.

AI will cut down a lot of your time in brainstorming and hashing out the video. If you're against using AI, you can always grind it out and do it the hard way. I can tell you from experience that it's no fun, especially when the video flops. Don't grind it out on your own, work with AI to cut down production time.

> *Just remember: AI gives you a starting point. It's your job to revise, test, and refine until it fits your brand and voice.*

Once you have your video search engine optimized, it's off to the races. The fun part about YouTube is that search traffic only makes up a fraction of all watch time hours on the platform. This means that the rest comes through other avenues, one being recommendation-based content. When you have a video that aligns closely with other videos in your genre, YouTube is more likely to recommend your video as the next option.

When viewers arrive on the YouTube home page, they'll see additional recommended videos. Do you remember your YouTube channel for research? Well, you were essentially training YouTube to serve you only videos within the genre you like, so that you primarily see relevant videos recommended all throughout the site.

FINDING THE RIGHT KEYWORDS FOR YOUR VIDEOS

You've already learned how to scope out the competition and uncover potential video concepts or ideas. To further expand your list of keywords to optimize your video, you can lean on YouTube's incognito mode. For those of you familiar with my keyword optimization process for Kindle Direct Publishing, you might see a parallel here.

Open a web browser in incognito mode and go to YouTube. This gives you unbiased search results and a clearer picture of how viable each keyword is. Start typing a single word from your keyword phrase and pause to see what YouTube suggests. Write down the top results. Build a deeper list by adding more words or cycling through the alphabet to explore variations.

For instance, if my keyword was "exercises for men", YouTube autosuggests:

- exercises for menopausal belly fat
- exercises for men over 50
- exercises for men's sexual health
- exercises for men over 60

- exercises for men over 70
- exercises for menopausal women

...and the list goes on.

Once I cycle through all those, I'll add a single letter of the alphabet after "exercises for men" and YouTube will serve other options.

When you have a few dozen keywords, look at how each one performs. Do an individual search of every relevant keyword on your list. Pay attention to the videos served up. Ask yourself these questions:

1. How long are the videos?
2. How many views does each video have?
3. When were the videos published?

If you see a video that catches your fancy, watch it. You get bonus points if you take the link and watch it with your new YouTube research account. That'll help further train the YouTube algorithm to show you nothing but the videos you want to publish.

Study the average video length and match it when you can (though it's not mandatory). When you find videos pulling thousands or hundreds of thousands of views, you know you're targeting a strong topic. Find ones uploaded within the past year to catch keywords that still perform well. Stay cautious with trends—building a video around a meme that faded a year ago usually backfires. Topics like that explode in the first few days, then disappear just as quickly.

Another gold mine for keyword research is the Analytics in YouTube Studio. Under Content, you'll find a section called "How viewers find your videos." Once you've had enough views, YouTube will display five different metrics of discovery:

1. **Overall**: Shows where your traffic is coming from, including YouTube search, external sites, suggested videos, and more.
2. **External**: Breaks down outside sources like Google Search, Facebook, or other websites that drive viewers to your channel.
3. **YouTube Search**: Reveals the exact keywords viewers use to find your videos. This is one of your most valuable keyword insights.
4. **Suggested Videos**: Lists the videos recommending your content. You'll often see your own videos here, which is helpful, but aim to get suggestions from other creators to expand your reach.
5. **Playlists**: Shows which playlists are generating views. Creating binge-worthy series helps increase watch time and keep viewers on your channel. More on playlists later.

YouTube Search is the tool you want to pay closest attention to. Double down on winning keywords by producing more videos that are relevant to that keyword phrase. When you have one video that performs well for a specific keyword, you're bound to capture the same, if not better, results for future videos.

What if you don't want to grind it out and find the keywords on your own? I ran into some challenges early on with YouTube and found tools like Morningfame, TubeBuddy, and VidIQ especially helpful. These services give video creators valuable insights into keywords, niche performance, and audience trends. They also highlight what other creators in your space are doing and offer helpful tools to support your channel's growth.

These days, I rarely rely on keyword research tools. After years of experience, I know my audience well and can handle research without using any paid platforms. If you're just starting out and want to save time while learning, investing in a tool might be worth it. Tools like TubeBuddy or VidIQ can offer helpful shortcuts, especially if you need support spotting trends, high-traffic keywords, or competitive gaps.

That said, these tools are not essential. Everything I've shared so far, along with what's still to come, will give you a strong foundation without spending a dime. If you're bootstrapping, stick with the free methods until your channel begins earning steady income. Once you reach $1,000 per month in revenue from affiliate sales, book sales, ads, or sponsorships, it makes sense to reinvest in a research tool. At that point, you're moving beyond the basics and focusing on growth.

They all come with free access, so visit the Resources in the back of this book. I've got one free month to Morningfame if you want to give it a shot. Avoid using the free trials until you're ready to publish videos consistently or have a deep backlist of content.

CRAFTING CLICKABLE TITLES WITHOUT LOSING RELEVANCE

Your title serves one primary function: getting the click. When viewers discover your video, they're provided with two pieces of information in the title and thumbnail. Yes, having relevant keywords in your title can make a difference in search and discovery. It's not the only factor in getting people to watch. Viewers must have a compelling reason to watch your video, and if you can't give them the right info, they're going to pass.

YouTube gives you up to 100 characters for your title, but I recommend using as few as necessary. In my experience, shorter titles perform best. They're easier to scan, which helps your video stand out from other options on the platform.

When I'm producing a title, I limit it to fifty to sixty characters, including spaces. I have had little success with emojis in titles, but don't let that stop you from experimenting with them. Those embellishments are possibly not what my audience prefers in their videos. Make every word count in your title. A small wording tweak can dramatically impact video viewership.

Creating a title comes back to understanding your audience. For me, I speak directly to authors, especially self-published or indie authors. I'll use terms my target audience is already searching. "Amazon KDP," "book marketing," and "Amazon Ads," are keywords I'll commonly use in my video titles. Also, when I'm producing these titles, I think of the experience level of my viewers as beginner to intermediate. I've really narrowed down my audience so that it's easier for me to create a title worth my viewer's attention.

I also anchor most of my titles in real-world pain points, such as no time, no money, or no results. Since I can provide a solution, I tap into those pain points to attract more viewers. The biggest key to success in my title selection is I lead with the keyword, then provide further context in the title and thumbnail. For example, I could use one of the previous terms in this title: *Amazon KDP: New Category Restrictions Could Get You Banned.*

Once I have a general idea of the video I'll shoot, I'll workshop titles and variations with AI. I provide all my requests to AI through a single prompt, so that it knows what I want and how I want it. I'll provide AI with this prompt:

Give me five compelling YouTube title variations based on this original title: Amazon KDP: New Category Restrictions Could Get You Banned. Keep the core topic and concept the same, but reword the titles to be more clickable and attention-grabbing. Each variation must include the keyword phrase 'Amazon KDP' and appeal to self-published authors concerned about platform policy changes.

Then it'll provide me with options like:

1. *Amazon KDP Category Rules Could Get You Banned*
2. *Amazon KDP Authors: Are You Breaking the New Category Rules?*
3. *New Amazon KDP Policy Could Wreck Your Publishing Account*
4. *Amazon KDP's New Category Crackdown: What Authors Must Know*
5. *The Hidden Amazon KDP Rule That Could Get You Removed*

From here, I pick apart the titles. If it feels even slightly off the mark for what I'll produce in the video, I discard it. When someone reads the title for a video, they must clearly understand what to expect. Unclear titles work only when the thumbnail provides the remaining context. Otherwise, viewers would pass on a good video with poor title choice.

Once you have a winning concept, keep AI on standby, because you're going to need to draft ideas for a thumbnail design, the second element that ties cohesively with a stellar title.

OPTIMIZING THUMBNAILS THAT GET CLICKED

The thumbnail is the graphic displayed alongside the title of your video when people discover your video. Ideally, you'll want the thumbnail to be sized 1280 by 720 pixels (16:9 ratio) and the file size can't be any larger than 2MB (megabytes).

Your video thumbnail should work collaboratively with the title, painting a compelling picture of why your video is worth watching over the other options on YouTube.

Fair warning: graphic design isn't something that comes to everyone right away. You can lean on free graphic design software like Canva, Book Brush, or even my preferred tool, GIMP (GNU Image Manipulation Program). You can use other premium software like Photoshop, but I wouldn't recommend investing in a subscription until you can afford that monthly expense. You do not have to be a graphic design wizard; you just need to learn as you go. Once you've gotten a few dozen videos under your belt, you'll find thumbnail design will come easier.

In the event you do not have the time or patience to create thumbnails, you can try one of three things:

1. **Use automatic screenshots.** YouTube provides three auto-generated captures to choose from. They're quick and easy but not always the most compelling.
2. **Hire a freelancer.** You'll find plenty of designers on platforms like Fiverr or Upwork charging $5 to $25. Provide direction and examples for best results.
3. **Generate art with AI tools.** Tools like Canva, Leonardo. Ai, and Midjourney can help you create custom thumbnails

that grab attention. Just make sure they're readable at a glance and fit your brand.

For authors who are on-screen talent, I recommend using your face on the thumbnail. It'll go a long way in branding and recognition. Based on your type of content, use a picture that reflects the tone or feel of the video.

A few years ago, I spent about two hours shooting various facial expressions. A quick Google search provided me with a list of facial expressions that I could use for future thumbnails. I easily snapped 100 pictures but removed about half of them because some had flaws in lighting, expression, or clarity.

You can do the same thing: schedule time to snap some pictures of yourself. Try to keep your hands free so that you can use them for expressive shots or directional gestures (i.e., pointing, counting, etc.). Most modern cameras have a timer feature, so set it for three to five seconds—enough time to strike a pose without feeling rushed. Don't stop to review each image right away. The goal is to capture a large batch first, then sort through them later to find the best options.

If you want to build visual consistency across your thumbnails and channel, consider wearing similar outfits or using props that reflect your genre or personality. For example, I often wear an orange shirt in my videos and thumbnails. It wasn't part of some master plan. I just kept doing it, and over time, it became something my audience recognized. You don't need to do the same thing, but think about how subtle, repeated visual cues might support your author brand over time.

When you have a stockpile of pictures, you can now import each one into your preferred graphic design software, where you can add:

- Text
- Visual elements like logos or clip art
- More contrast and deeper color saturation
- Optional: Remove the background, leaving only you in the picture

Any authors that are producing faceless videos will have to rely on the other elements in the previous list to do the heavy lifting.

Remember that composition makes all the difference, so place your elements wisely on the thumbnail. For text, I avoid putting it over vital elements that communicate what the video is about without saying a word. This means don't put text over your face or covering your body if you're using your hands to express an emotion. Also, be mindful of where your eyes are tracking. If you're looking to the right or left, place your image strategically so that you appear to be looking at the title or the focal point of the thumbnail.

When researching your niche, you should've seen common thumbnails used. Note any other graphic elements to include and build a composition that embodies the best of those thumbnails while showcasing you and your personality.

YouTube has a thumbnail split test feature you can run on long form videos. Split testing has yet to roll out for YouTube Shorts and Live videos, but I'm sure it'll come in due time. For now, you can upload two to three thumbnail variations to split test. Once you publish a video, YouTube tests variations of your thumbnail to see which one gets the most clicks and holds viewers' attention the longest. It's not just about getting a click. You want people to stick around and watch as much of the video as possible.

After a two-week test, the thumbnail that performs the best will be the winner. In the event the test is inconclusive, YouTube will select one thumbnail. I recommend setting a reminder for the day your split test ends so you can review the results, analyze the data, and adjust future thumbnails based on what you learn.

I cannot overstate this enough: the greatest barrier of entry to success on YouTube is the title and thumbnail. Before you ever shoot a single video, lock those items in, then produce a video around the concept. It'll keep you dialed in while shooting the video and get you truly focused on delivering the best possible video that honors what the viewers expect after seeing your title and thumbnail.

The next great hurdle is producing a video that keeps people watching, but that'll take time and practice as mentioned before. However, it doesn't end there. We still have one untapped area that could take your video from miring in obscurity to discoverable through YouTube search, and various search engines like Google, DuckDuckGo, Bing, and more.

SMART DESCRIPTION WRITING THAT ACTUALLY HELPS

Writing descriptions is much easier now than when I first started. Back then, YouTube experts advised cramming in as many keywords as possible or even pasting the full video script. Just because YouTube allows up to 5,000 characters doesn't mean you need to use them all.

Let's start with the basics first. Visit YouTube Studio on desktop and select **Settings** on the left menu. Select **Upload defaults** where you can put in relevant links and details about you as an author. My upload default for descriptions is the following.

- The Self-Publishing Hub – https://TheSelfPublishingHub.com

- Subscribe to my email newsletter – https://DaleLinks.com/SignUp

- Join Channel Memberships – https://www.youtube.com/channel/UCKv8xcrFntOERL7NUXgkypg/join

- Join my Discord community – http://dalelinks.com/discord

- Check out my podcast channel – https://www.youtube.com/@selfpubwithdale

- My Books – https://DaleLinks.com/MyBooks

- Wanna tip me? Visit https://dalelroberts.gumroad.com/coffee.

Where noted, some outbound links financially benefit the channel through affiliate programs. I only endorse programs, products, or services I use and can stand confidently behind. These links do not affect your purchase price and help build and grow this channel. Thanks in advance for understanding!

-Dale L. Roberts

This provides viewers with all they need to know about me and my business. I provide all the relevant links and an affiliate disclosure. If you don't plan on doing affiliate marketing, you don't have to include a disclosure. I place one in every video just to be safe since I sometimes will mention a product in the video. This keeps my content compliant with the FTC.

> *Side note: The FTC, or Federal Trade Commission, is a U.S. government agency that enforces laws against deceptive advertising and marketing practices. It's important for video creators who use affiliate links because the FTC requires them to disclose any financial relationships with companies promoting products or services. This means you must inform your audience if you earn a commission from purchases made through your affiliate links. This transparency helps maintain trust with viewers, promotes ethical marketing practices, and complies with legal guidelines to avoid penalties.*

When you're ready to publish a video, your default info will already be in place. All you need to do is add a short, relevant paragraph and any links you mentioned in the video. You'll notice I lean heavily in favor of less is more.

According to the YouTube Liaison Rene Ritchie, one mind behind YouTube, the description is merely there to provide context for the video. You can include keywords if they're relevant, but it's not a deal-breaker.

Limit your paragraph to only three to four sentences and lead with a great hook. Since YouTube truncates descriptions after the first two lines, you have very little real estate to tell viewers what your video is all about. Get to the point, right away in the description.

To level up the likelihood of search and discovery, you can always tap into additional keyword opportunities in time stamps. You can segment parts of your video so that viewers can skip to or easily find what they need.

It seems counter-intuitive to provide viewers the opportunity to skip portions of your video, but it works out rather nice for being discoverable. For instance, I have a weekly news segment on my podcast. Each news item carries some trending topic or keyword, so I'll create the time stamps like this:

0:00 Intro
0:29 Sponsor
1:49 If You're an Author, Don't Fall for This Scam
5:54 Spotify Expands Its Audiobooks Offering To Listeners In Germany, Austria, Switzerland, and Liechtenstein
7:30 AppSumo presents DepositPhotos
9:23 IngramSpark presents Tertulia for Authors
11:08 AMPlify Audiobooks
13:10 StoryOrigin presents Beyond Distribution: Building a Strategic Roadmap for Success
13:41 Authors Guild presents How to Book Podcasts as an Author
14:23 The Secrets of Successful Author Branding w/ Bryan Cohen
14:55 Author Nation tickets
15:45 Kitboga: Scammers Panic Exposed on Live Video
16:40 Closing

YouTube makes the timestamps clickable, allowing people to jump straight to a specific section. It also adds visual segments in the video pane, making it easy to drag the slider to the part they want to watch.

Having these timestamps isn't a necessity, but they can go a long way for some authors who want even a few extra views or watch time hours. Every bit counts. Try it out to see how it works for you. Some types of video content don't need timestamps, so use your discretion.

Based on my earlier advice, you'll want to share a link to the hand-off video from the end screen. This helps some viewers who aren't quick enough to click on the end screen elements. And it also helps with viewers who stop watching early. If you've got the answer to their problems, chances are likely they might not even make it to the end of the video. Give them the opportunity to see the video through your description.

I lean heavily on AI to help draft a killer description that includes relevant keywords. I'll provide all the keywords I want, and details about how I prefer my descriptions. Then, I ask it to provide additional tags for the video with up to 500 characters in total. I continue to use tags for backup despite their ineffectiveness. Ask AI to give you a paragraph of relevant keywords separated by commas. Then, copy and paste that paragraph into the tags section.

Don't overthink tags; they're really not that big of a deal. I've had many videos perform well without tags. It's not a point to stress over.

Simply put, your video description doesn't need to be perfect, it just needs to include keywords naturally. There's no secret formula for writing one that converts. Keep it simple and focus your energy on strong content, a compelling title, and an eye-catching thumbnail. Everything else comes second.

CHAPTER 5:
BUILDING A LOYAL AUDIENCE AND ENGAGED COMMUNITY

I've been a huge fan and avid user of YouTube well before I even imagined uploading videos or earning money from doing it. The part I loved most about YouTube was the ability to chat with my favorite YouTubers through their video comments. There's something quite special about leaving a comment on a video and getting a reply from the creator. When was the last time you could watch a movie, leave a comment on it, and have a famous actor respond to it? That's the feeling I would get when I'd get a notification on YouTube that someone responded to my comment.

Getting a comment from another viewer was just icing on the cake. It's nice to know that I'm not the only one interested in and engaged in a video or its creator. Having recognizable names from within a tight-knit community on YouTube goes a long way in me returning to watch future videos.

Nothing used to frustrate me more than when a video creator ignored my comment, especially when I asked a legitimate question or raised a valid concern. It takes only a moment to reply, and with YouTube's built-in tools for quick responses, creators have little excuse. At the very least, they can click the heart icon to show the commenter their message mattered.

When I first started on YouTube, I promised myself I'd never get too big to reply to comments or engage with viewers. After all, they're the reason your channel grows in the first place. That belief was reinforced when I spoke with viral video creator and hybrid-published author Evan Carmichael. His inspirational, binge-worthy content brings in tons of views, watch time, and, naturally, a steady stream of comments.

During a conference presentation, Evan shared his approach to handling comments. He made it clear that every comment gets a reply, and he even hired a team to help manage them. When a comment was aggressive or confrontational, he had the team forward it directly to him. He trained them to handle the day-to-day engagement but took on the tougher conversations himself.

I don't expect everyone to subscribe to the same belief that Evan and I do, but even if you adopt a fraction of this philosophy, you'll have a greater advantage over creators who don't even give their comments a second look.

WHY ENGAGEMENT IS MORE POWERFUL THAN VIEWS

In January 2018, YouTube rolled out the current requirements to qualify for their YouTube Partner program. Prior to that roll out, creators could coast by on views alone. The problem was that anyone could get views, but only truly gifted video creators could keep viewers watching. As mentioned previously, YouTube is all about viewers staying longer on their site, watching videos and seeing ads.

The platform can't make money on free views alone, that's why they have ads on videos, so that they can offset costs for video hosting, site maintenance, among other expenses.

Don't stress about view counts, that part comes with time and consistency. Instead, focus on making each viewer count. Start by encouraging interaction. When people engage with your content, they're more likely to return for future videos. Simple actions, like replying to comments, can even bring them back to the same video, boosting watch time and signaling relevance to YouTube's algorithm.

Building a community involves much more than just asking for and replying to comments. To truly engage your audience, you'll need to tap into other aspects of community building on YouTube. Let's explore some of the most effective strategies.

ENCOURAGING COMMENTS AND FEEDBACK

We've already discussed various ways you should and shouldn't conduct yourself on video. One item I mentioned was limiting your call-to-action, so you don't split the viewers' attention. Avoid saying "subscribe, like, comment, and share" because most viewers won't do any of those things since you've provided them with a to-do list of *your* needs.

Instead, get razor sharp on your CTA. Any time I have the opportunity, I will ask for a comment. Be prepared, because you might not agree with some answers you get. But when you ask, expect an answer.

For instance, if I were producing a video about Amazon KDP's Terms and Conditions, I could ask viewers:

CHAPTER 5: BUILDING A LOYAL AUDIENCE AND ENGAGED COMMUNITY

Have you ever read Amazon KDP's Terms and Conditions? If so, do you think they're confusing or misleading? Let me know in the comments.

Keep your CTA brief and to the point. You know you have the right question when the comments come pouring in. Starting out, it's going to be hard knowing what will draw more comments, so don't lose heart. Produce the videos as if you're speaking to 100,000 people so that when you finally hit that major milestone, you'll already have best practices in place.

Schedule time once per week to answer comments meaningfully. You could spend every day answering comments, but it can chip away at your time, leaving you less time to focus on your author career. Instead, pick one day at a specific hour that you only reply to comments.

YouTube Studio provides a filter for viewer comments. Start with the filter set to "I haven't responded" under **Response status**. Respond to your comments and if you run into someone who you disagree with, remember, that doesn't mean you have to start an argument. Express your appreciation that they watched the video and left a comment. I'll address trolls and critics later in the chapter.

For new YouTubers, I recommend keeping the conversation going. Answer the original comment, then ask a question pertinent to the topic. The real trick is keeping an eye out for additional responses in a comment thread.

Change the filter for comments to "Responses with new replies", then you'll get a full list of conversations you started, and that have continued. If you have less than 1,000 subscribers, I recommend stretching out those conversations as long as they can go.

Don't force it, though. Should a viewer post a comment like, "Great video," a simple thanks and a heart on the comment goes a long way.

Some creators believe that videos with more comments is more likely to be promoted by YouTube. While the algorithm is complex and YouTube hasn't confirmed whether comments alone have a direct impact, engagement signals as a whole—watch time, likes, comments, and shares—do play a role in how your video performs. Encouraging meaningful conversation in your comments isn't just about building community. It might also give your video a subtle boost.

As you're going through your comments, pay close attention to questions, ideas, and suggestions, because this intel can go a long way for future video projects. Some of my best video ideas were crowd-sourced. All it took was managing the comments and interacting in meaningful ways.

POSTS TAB CONTENT THAT WORKS

Posts is a featured tab on every YouTube channel where the video creator can post:

- Text-based content
- Images and GIFs
- Quizzes
- Polls

I've had a lot of success using the **Posts** tab (formerly known as the Community tab) over the past several years. This tool helps you keep your current subscribers engaged while also attracting new ones. In fact, I was getting three to eight new subscribers from these posts. Apparently, what I was posting was a hit. You can create a post either directly from the YouTube homepage or through YouTube Studio. If you choose Studio, click "Create" then "Create Post" to be redirected to the same posting interface on YouTube.

Here's how I did it.

Once a week, spend ten to fifteen minutes to schedule the next seven days' worth of posts. When you're first doing this, you might only get one or two posts out per week and that's okay. The point isn't to bog you down with being efficient early on. Learn the posting process, then scale as you get acclimated to the layout.

Go back to my earlier recommendations about producing content that attracts your ideal viewer. You're going to apply the same principles here.

Here's a sample of my current posting schedule:

- **Sunday: Quiz Time** – A publishing-related quiz, sometimes focused on specific tools or industry trivia, designed to educate and entertain.
- **Monday: 6 or Fewer Words** – A weekly challenge to write a story, scene, or idea in six words or fewer, often themed around writing, regret, triumph, or horror.
- **Tuesday: Poll** – A thought-provoking question about book marketing, publishing tactics, or author habits that sparks discussion and insight.
- **Wednesday: Pop Quiz** – A quick multiple-choice question covering self-publishing, book platforms, or writing tools.

- **Thursday: Wrong Answers** – A funny, low-pressure prompt inviting ridiculous responses based on a writing- or publishing-related phrase.
- **Friday: Poll** – A second weekly poll, often focused on book production, distribution, advertising, or business strategy.
- **Saturday: Interview Deck** – An open-ended, conversation-starting question. It can be fun, serious, or reflective—perfect for community bonding.

This schedule came from a lot of experimentation and continued changes and improvements. I discovered quickly that my ideal viewers loved quizzes, polls, and any writing prompt challenge. For anyone new to YouTube, lean on polls and quizzes at first; they're dead simple to put together and can be fun for the random YouTube viewer browsing the site.

As I've mentioned before, use AI to help brainstorm a daily, weekly, or monthly posting schedule. You'll get far more done than you would working alone. I've trained AI on my content, so it can generate quizzes and polls based on my videos and books. From there, I promote everything more organically. My goal is for posts to feel like a conversation, not just another book promo.

The results will be slow at first, but when you stick to it for a few months at a time, you will see exponential growth through **Posts**. I've had some viewers stumble on my posts and just binge on the quizzes, polls, and writing prompts. It's incredible to see one person dominating my comments feed because of their excitement in this part of my community.

Are **Posts** mandatory for you to grow a community on YouTube? No, in fact, I know of many successful video creators who never use it. From first-hand experience, the **Posts** tab has been instrumental in my growth on YouTube and continues to be a staple of my content.

LIVESTREAMS THAT BUILD TRUST AND CONNECTION

The single most effective tool in rapid audience growth is live video. For one, it's dead simple to livestream video compared to having to record, edit, and publish it. Next, technology has advanced so much over the past several years that anyone with an internet connection can win big with the right hardware. Last, livestreaming is how you can interact directly with your viewing audience, getting near real-time feedback.

One of the sweetest parts about livestreaming is that you can plan however much you want in advance for the broadcast. Unlike pre-recorded videos, you only get one take, so make it a good one.

Don't stress over being perfect live; just strive to be better. For now, your mission should be to connect with your live viewers. But you also must remember that you'll get fewer people watching live than you will with replays. How you structure your live videos makes all the difference in getting and retaining your viewership.

When I go live every Monday at 6:15 p.m. EDT on my podcast channel, I structure it like this:

1. **Start with a hold screen**: This gives viewers time to join before the main content begins.
2. **Confirm the livestream is active**: I check YouTube to make sure everything is running properly.

3. **Switch to the camera**: Once confirmed, I transition from the hold screen to my on-screen intro.
4. **Record the main audio podcast**: This is the core content of the live show.
5. **Pause for live chat** – After recording the main segment, I hang out with viewers in the chat. This is my favorite part—it's where I get to catch up with familiar faces.
6. **Record the news segment**: I shift gears and capture the week's self-publishing news for the audio version.
7. **Clip and schedule the news**: After the stream, I edit the news segment into its own video and schedule it for release the next day.
8. **Edit the main podcast replay**: One day later, I trim the livestream to isolate the main podcast segment, giving both pieces room to shine.

Some viewers asked why I clip that live footage, and the reason is simple: being there for the live show is better than watching the replay. Viewers can lose some of that sense of connection through video replays. I discovered unedited videos received criticism of being too long-winded or rambling. I took it to heart and solved the problem. It paid off in dividends.

I created a can't-miss livestream environment that viewers want to be part of, especially if they're looking to get answers or entertainment.

Livestreaming can be daunting, at first, since you're essentially performing without a net. Thankfully, you're not doing a high stakes trapeze act, so give yourself some grace and allow for some mistakes to happen. Let's start with the path of least resistance: the software you'll need for livestreaming.

Companies like StreamYard, Restream, and eCamm provide services for livestreaming to multiple platforms like YouTube, Facebook, X, LinkedIn, and more. Even if you can't afford the premium subscription services, these companies have a free model that's more than sufficient for the budding livestreamer.

Anyone who has a firmer grasp on tech can lean on more advanced livestreaming software like OBS (Open Broadcaster Software), a free program that comes with a steep learning curve. I've been using OBS for years now and know my way around fairly well. However, it's not for the faint of heart and requires time to test and learn. Unlike the browser-based livestreaming services mentioned previously, OBS has far more flexibility and provides users with granular control of their broadcasts.

Run a few test streams before creating an official event and inviting your viewers to come join you. Get a few friends to help you for a test stream. You'll want to create an event through the Go live option in the top right corner of YouTube Studio. You can either go live right away or schedule a stream. I recommend the latter because it gives you time to experiment with settings. Keep in mind, you can literally go live through a scheduled event any time you want. When you set up an event, you'll get a shareable link. If you set the event as Public, everyone will see a thumbnail and title for your show. If you're really fancy, you could post a video teaser that runs until the time of the event.

When you go live, take a deep breath and remember to have fun. Everyone starts at zero, so don't let that discourage you from carrying on a conversation with yourself or the viewers who watch on the replay. Always broadcast like you're talking to 100,000 people, because one day, it just might reach that many viewers.

Stacking onto what you've learned so far, you can combine **Posts** and livestreaming together. Promote your event on your **Posts** with a fun quiz or poll (don't forget to include a CTA with the link). And, if you're livestreaming, you can forward viewers to your **Posts** to vote on the latest poll or answer a quiz.

Livestreaming is, by far, one of my most favorite aspects of being a video content creator. It challenges me to be a better speaker and video producer. Every time I'm done with a livestream, I'm exhausted but happy. Usually, within the first day, I'll go back and briefly review my footage, take notes, and make a few adjustments for future broadcasts.

NAVIGATING CRITICISM, TROLLS, AND PUBLIC FEEDBACK

You will run into negative feedback and outright trolls, but don't lose faith. There are truly more good people than bad on the platform. If you've done everything you can to provide the absolute best video and interaction every time, then any detractors can take a backseat. This is your journey, so you get to choose the narrative.

I know plenty of content creators who enjoy engaging with trolls and sometimes even turn them into loyal viewers or superfans (see my earlier story about Evan Carmichael). Personally, I don't have the time or patience for that kind of back-and-forth.

Before you publish your first video, decide how you'll handle trolls. And to be clear, I'm not talking about people who simply disagree with you. Disagreements are normal, trolling is something else entirely.

I have zero tolerance for cursing, name-calling, or unfounded accusations. My community is meant to be family-friendly, supportive, and uplifting. Being an author is already tough, so I make no room for toxic behavior that drags others down. Still, not every negative comment is trolling. Someone might say your audio is too quiet or your pacing feels off. It might sting, but if there's no malice, that kind of feedback can help you grow. When a comment crosses into personal attacks or hate, block it. If it's just blunt but honest, take a breath, consider the note, and decide if it's useful.

When you see a comment like that, do yourself a favor: don't respond and block the person. Click the three dots below the comment and select "Hide user from channel." The blocked user can still watch your videos and comment, but no one will ever see their comments.

Arguing with negative viewers isn't worth your energy. Focus instead on creating for the people who appreciate your message. Your time is better spent engaging with those who support your work—not those trying to tear it down.

Just as trolls are inevitable, so are bots and scammers. You can block that user, but an even better feature awaits you: Report. This function allows you to notify YouTube that you have a spammer on your hands. Do not use this feature as a retaliation for a disagreement. The report feature is for comments that contain:

- Unwanted commercial content or spam
- Pornography or sexually explicit material
- Child abuse
- Hate speech or graphic violence
- Promotes terrorism

- Harassment or bullying
- Suicide or self-injury
- Misinformation

Sure, some trolls qualify for reporting since harassment or bullying is on the list. I give the commenter the benefit of the doubt. They might be having a tough go at life, and I was the person caught in their crosshairs. I give trolls a pass and just block them. But scammers, spammers, and bots? Not a chance!

Do not allow spam comments to permeate your community. You never know when someone stumbles over a spam comment and clicks on a link or finds an illicit site. Take care of the problem right away so it doesn't harm your viewers.

Even if you ignore my advice about replying to comments, at least take care of the spam. Someone has to take the trash out, and unfortunately, that's you. YouTube does a decent job of sending spammers to your **Held** tab, but plenty still slip through.

Keep an eye out for repeated keywords or phrases you want filtered. Head to **Settings** in the bottom-left corner of YouTube Studio, then select **Community**. Scroll down to **Blocked words** and enter any terms you want automatically flagged. YouTube will immediately route comments containing those words to the **Held** section. From there, you decide what to do with them.

The twenty-four-hour rule has never failed me. If a comment gets under my skin, I give it a day before responding. That pause helps me come up with a reply that's meaningful, constructive, and professional. If I can't offer a thoughtful response, I'll often just thank them for watching and move on. You don't have to do the same, but be warned, arguing with someone in the comments rarely ends well. The internet has a long memory. One heated reply can overshadow months of goodwill and hurt your credibility with your actual audience. Plenty of creators have learned this the hard way. Don't let a moment of frustration derail the reputation you've worked so hard to build.

Give the other person the benefit of the doubt, because you might misinterpret a comment and unintentionally overreact. Ask the commenter for more details or to restate what they said so you clearly understand what they're communicating.

Jamie Jasta, lead singer of the heavy metal band Hatebreed, once shared how he disarms hostile commenters with a simple question: "Are you okay?" That one line often shifts the tone entirely, turning angry viewers into calm, even compliant, commenters. It won't work every time. Some people just aren't open to reason, but it's a powerful reminder not to take negativity personally.

> One of the most rewarding aspects of growing my YouTube channels is the community that's come with it. I never would've guessed that other people would nerd out about the same stuff I do, and want to keep doing it with me for years. It's like having an extended family. I never tire of seeing familiar people in the comments, where they share their updates and latest wins.

That's the most valuable part of YouTube: community. When you show up consistently, stay genuine, and create a space where people feel like they belong, it becomes one of the best time investments you can make.

CHAPTER 6:
CONVERTING VIEWERS INTO READERS & BOOK BUYERS

Even though I'd launched my first YouTube channel in April 2016 and my second YouTube channel in June 2019, I had yet to write and publish a book for my audience. I had such a deep back list of fitness books, but none of that would appeal to my viewing audience. Yes, I'd sold my fair share of online courses and consultation packages while raking in affiliate and sponsorship revenue. However, my viewers never truly had a book they could sink their teeth into…that is, until August 2020.

I started writing with purpose, focusing on content that would serve my viewers and complement my YouTube videos. When I released the first of six books on writing and self-publishing, it quickly became clear how eager my audience was to hear from me in the book world.

Within the first month of launch, sales surged and reviews poured in, all because I used my YouTube platform to promote books for authors. Of course, it wasn't as simple as showing up and asking viewers to buy.

Every action was intentional and meant to build trust with my audience. I never published a video, email broadcast, or social media post without thinking about:

1. Delivering value first.
2. Solving a serious problem for authors.
3. Naturally integrating my books into each video.

Never blindly jump into promoting your book without first delivering something truly valuable for your ideal viewer. Otherwise, when you ask for viewers to buy your book, everything else might appear disingenuous. First, think about a problem your viewer has, then decide how you can fulfill that need. Then, wow your viewers with high-value content that easily integrates your book. This means you want to avoid any surprise calls-to-action and don't produce a mid-roll ad, because you will most certainly lose watch time.

Some viewers won't wait around for a mid-roll pitch about your book. Taking a cue from Ten Hundred (as mentioned earlier), you can find natural ways to transition into promoting it. Often, it doesn't take much. Share the book in a way that fits the flow of your video without breaking momentum.

We've only briefly covered the concept of using video to market and promote your books. Let's take a more granular look and some potential options you can consider for future video productions.

INTEGRATING YOUR BOOK INTO THE CONTENT NATURALLY

We already know that when I produce a video, I go in with a strong understanding of what outcome I want to have. If my primary goal is to sell more books, I think about how I can craft a conversation around the core content of a specific publication.

For example, how I promote *Amazon Keywords for Books* could include these video concepts:

1. *Why Your Book Isn't Ranking on Amazon*

- Concept: Break down how Amazon's search algorithm works, what actually moves the needle, and how most authors are using keywords wrong.
- Natural plug: Walk viewers through one of the keyword planning techniques from my book and explain how to test terms before publishing.

2. *I Tried Amazon Ads with No Keywords—Here's What Happened*

- Concept: A challenge-style experiment where I run two ad sets—one using strategic keywords, the other with auto targeting—and compare results.
- Natural plug: Highlight how keyword research improves ad ROI and mention my book as the resource that teaches my exact system.

3. *Top 5 or Top 10 Keyword Mistakes Killing Your Book Sales*

- Concept: Myth-busting rant that hits the biggest traps authors fall into, like irrelevant keywords, keyword stuffing, or ignoring backend fields.
- Natural plug: Position my book as the go-to solution

for avoiding these traps and building smarter keyword foundations.

4. *How to Make Your Book Discoverable Without Ads*

- Concept: Teach how keywords, metadata, and product page structure all work together to generate organic sales, especially for low-budget authors.
- Natural plug: Explain how my book's strategy helps authors gain visibility organically, even without ads.

5. *The Amazon Keyword Strategy I Wish I Knew Sooner*

- Concept: A personal, reflective video where I talk about my early mistakes and the moment I realized how Amazon's system *really* works.
- Natural plug: Position my book as the culmination of hard-earned lessons and the guide I wish I had back then.

These examples aren't perfect; I can still sharpen and improve them. They show exactly how I approach each video, focusing on three key elements:

- Crafting a clickable title
- Choosing a winning concept that addresses a major pain point
- Finding a natural place to mention my book

I'm still focused on selling books, but I have to be realistic, not everyone watches every video. Avoid creating content solely for your existing subscribers. Instead, aim to attract a broader segment of your ideal audience. That mindset is the key to long-term growth.

Just because I know some fiction authors are curious about how that works for them, here's how I'd promote my sci-fi horror series *Infestate*:

1. *Why Malls Make the Perfect Horror Setting (And Why We're Afraid of Them)*

   - Concept: A breakdown of why enclosed spaces like malls fuel dread in horror fiction—touch on nostalgia, consumerism, and isolation.
   - Plug: Share how *Infestate* uses the mall setting to trap characters in escalating terror. Mention how I subverted mall tropes with creature horror.

2. *What Makes a Sci-Fi Creature Truly Terrifying?*

   - Concept: Compare famous creatures (The Thing, Aliens/Xenomorph, Cloverfield) and analyze what makes them effective: biology, intelligence, unpredictability.
   - Plug: Reveal my creature design inspiration in *Infestate* and how I made my monsters psychologically unnerving—not just gory.

3. *These 3 Sci-Fi Horror Tropes Still Work (When Done Right)*

   - Concept: Discuss overused vs. effective tropes (i.e., infection outbreaks, unreliable survivors, paranoia). Include examples from media that fans will know.

- Plug: Use scenes from *Infestate* to show how I twisted familiar tropes—like a drugged-out hustler or emotionally broken survivor—into something fresh.

4. *How I Turned an Ordinary Mall into a Living Nightmare*

- Concept: A behind-the-scenes "author story" that feels like a confession or creative process deep-dive. Readers *love* origin stories.
- Plug: Share how *Infestate* was born, maybe inspired by lock-downs, consumer chaos, or fear of enclosed spaces. Mention the awards casually as part of the book's journey.

5. *The 10 Best Sci-Fi Horror Stories You've Never Heard Of*

- Concept: A recommendation list (YouTube loves these). Shine light on underrated or indie sci-fi horror stories from books, games, and films.
- Plug: End the list with *Infestate* as my passion project. "I'd be a fool not to mention this one. It's mine, and it has scared the hell out of my readers."

Again, these rough examples are great jumping-off points, but nothing that I'd execute on without a little research in advance. To be clear, I wouldn't post these sci-fi horror videos onto my current YouTube channels devoted to writing and publishing. I'd probably create a new channel dedicated solely to sci-fi horror books, shows, and movies.

Mentioning your book doesn't have to be an elaborate stage show with months of preparation. You can transition into mentioning your book subtly. For instance, if I did the first video from my self-publishing content list, I'd produce it something like this:

1. Lead with a hook.
2. Deliver the goods.
3. Find a perfect spot to mention my book.
4. Deliver even more of the goods.
5. Finish the video.

That script could look something like this:

> *Keyword research doesn't have to be overwhelming or time consuming if you have a few safeguards in place and a rough understanding of the topic. I dive deeper into keyword research in my five-time award-winning book Amazon Keywords for Books. Grab a copy at any online retailer or library at DaleLinks.com/KeywordsBook.*

It wasn't complicated and didn't rely on clever tactics to work. I delivered value to the viewer and kept the CTA simple and direct. By getting straight to the point, I leave less room for viewers to skip ahead.

You've already seen how links to your book can appear in the video, description, and pinned comment. Once you're eligible for the YouTube Partner Program, you can also add clickable end screens. These let you display your book or another video during the final seconds, offering one more way to guide your viewers.

Experiment with how and when you mention your book in a video. It doesn't always need to be a CTA. You might casually highlight a review, mention an award, or read a short passage as part of the content. Once viewers understand what your book offers, many will start looking for it.

When you mention a book in your video, be intentional about it. I see a bump in sales every time I reference one of my titles on camera. Instead of a vague line like "Check out all my books at XYZ.com," I aim for a specific, relevant mention tied to the video content.

Vague requests get vague results. Be bold and just ask. Or give your viewers an undeniable reason to buy your book right away.

BUILDING A SIMPLE VIEWER FUNNEL

Imagine not only making book sales but also earning additional revenue beyond that. What if I told you it's not essential to promote your book in every single video? In fact, there's a much better way to connect with your audience while protecting your overall author brand.

Enter email marketing.

Every author needs an email list to thrive in today's market, especially if they're independent or self-published. Running a solo business is hard enough as it is, now adding to the stress is the worry of losing even one reader or viewer.

This is where you should have some best practices in place for collecting emails and communicating with your valued email subscribers. Unlike YouTube, you won't have to appease any algorithms in order to reach your viewers.

Anytime you launch a new book, you'll have an email list to share it with. You can also promote current videos or upcoming projects to build hype and generate more sales and revenue.

Instead of mentioning your book in a video, try promoting your email newsletter. Again, lead with value, solve a problem, then go for the ask. Keep your CTA brief but also give viewers a very compelling reason to join your email newsletter.

For example:

> *Want insider tips on self-publishing, book marketing, and making more sales—without the fluff? Join my free weekly newsletter for authors and get real strategies that actually work—delivered straight to your inbox. Subscribe today at DaleLinks.com/SignUp.*

If I want to do something for my sci-fi horror brand, it could be something like:

> *Love stories where science meets terror? Join my free newsletter for sci-fi horror fans and get early access to twisted tales, exclusive drops, and behind-the-scenes madness. Subscribe at DaleLewisRoberts.com/Signup.*

You can sweeten the deal and give your viewers an offer they can't refuse: the reader magnet. This item, also known as a lead magnet or bribe, entices readers to join your email list. Keep it simple, though. Create a reader magnet that is a perfect companion to your brand.

For my nonfiction brand, my reader magnets could be a checklist, top 10 list for authors, an Amazon Ads tutorial, a seven-day writing challenge, and more. My fiction brand could use prequels, sequels, spin-offs, and even samples to entice more subscribers. Test out a variety of different reader magnet types to see what draws the most subscribers. Then, double down on pushing that lead magnet or creating more just like it.

Once a subscriber is in your email ecosystem, all bets are off. You now have free rein over what you do and when. However, I highly recommend setting up automation so that new subscribers get a sequence of emails that further establish your authority in your niche. Part of that automation must include your books.

Instead of beating up your subscribers and demanding they buy your book, lean on some third-party credibility. You can share snippets of a review, showcase an award you won, or even how you developed your fiction work. Once you've provided value, asking for them to check out your book gets a lot easier.

Viral social media star and former guest of my podcast, Brad Gosse, once shared how he gets a bump in sales every time he shares negative, one-star reviews.[iii] This feedback would normally break most authors, but for Brad, he saw an opportunity to get a few laughs while drawing attention to his books. He promoted his book by sharing a negative review, and his diehard fans respond by buying the book and leaving positive reviews, all without him ever asking.

There's no one way to promote your book through email marketing, so if you haven't implemented an email list in your marketing and promotional strategy, now is a good time to do so. And don't worry, every author starts with zero subscribers. It takes time, patience, and a whole lot of experimentation.

You can leverage your email list in several powerful ways:

- **Recruit beta readers**: Get early feedback before launch.
- **Build an ARC team**: Send advance copies to trusted readers who leave reviews on launch day.
- **Newsletter swaps**: Partner with other authors to promote each other's books.
- **Promote a book launch**: Drive awareness and early sales from your most loyal readers.
- **Direct sales**: Skip the middleman and keep more of your revenue.
- **Push affiliate products**: Recommend tools, services, or books you trust. When someone clicks your link and buys, you earn a commission.

Every author, regardless of genre, experience, or platform, should build an email list. It remains one of the most powerful tools for marketing your books, connecting with readers, and creating long-term success. Start building it now, and you'll thank yourself later.

TRACKING WHAT WORKS

Even after getting this far, it's normal to wonder whether these strategies are actually working. Tracking sales is part of the process, but there are plenty of tools available to make it easier.

Start by creating a universal link, so any time you mention your book, you can quickly direct viewers to it. Free tools like Books2Read and BookLinker let readers choose their favorite retailer and automatically route them to the right regional store.

When promoting your book, keep in mind that your audience may be global. Using a .com link can leave international readers struggling to find the right store. If someone outside the U.S. can't easily access your listing, you risk losing the sale. The more friction you create, the faster potential readers move on.

Once you've created a universal book link, set up one of the following to make it easier to share:

1. **Custom domain**: A unique, branded URL purchased just for one book or series (e.g., MyBookTitle.com) that redirects to your sales or signup page.
2. **Subdomain**: A prefix that replaces the "www" on your main domain, ideal for organizing content by book, tool, or offer (e.g., Checklist.DaleLinks.com).
3. **Subdirectory**: A simple addition to the end of your existing domain, great for grouping all your links under one brand (e.g., DaleLinks.com/Checklist).

Using the original link created by Books2Read or BookLinker is okay, but it usually comes out as unmemorable and reads like alphabet soup. That's why you want to have a URL that redirects to that link.

I prefer setting up subdirectory URLs because it builds awareness of my site and also provides something easy for anyone to remember. When I have a good idea of the subdirectory I want to create, I use a free WordPress plug-in called Pretty Links. All I have to do is provide the universal book link and the word for the subdirectory, then I have a memorable link to share everywhere.

The beauty of using both universal book links and a redirect is that you can see precisely how many people are clicking on your link. For subdirectories, Pretty Links tracks both total and unique clicks, giving you a clear picture of how your link is performing. This'll indicate how many people are clicking and how often they are clicking on it.

Universal book link providers will give you the data on what marketplaces people clicked on in a given time period. This data will help inform you where you readers prefer buying books, therefore giving you the precise information of where you need to double down on your marketing efforts.

For example, here's how my universal link for *Self-Publishing for New Authors* has performed:

UNIVERSAL BOOK LINK RESULTS

- 5,632 total views
- 718 total clicks
- Amazon received over 50% of the clicks across ebook, paperback, and hardcover
- Apple Books accounted for 5% of total clicks
- Kobo brought in 2.5%
- Other retailers and libraries ranged from 1 to 12 clicks each

CHAPTER 6: CONVERTING VIEWERS INTO READERS & BOOK BUYERS

PRETTY LINKS RESULTS

- 2,536 total clicks
- 2,220 unique clicks

This information tells me that my subdirectory gets about half of the total clicks of the universal book link, so the link is drawing more readers beyond just what I've shared. Maybe readers are discovering this universal book link through my website or in the back of my book that's distributed through Draft2Digital. These links are generated through Draft2Digital's service, Books2Read, which makes it easy to share one link that works across platforms and countries.

However, that's not the end of it, because universal book link companies allow you to insert affiliate IDs into the backend, so that any time someone buys your book, you get an additional kickback. This could include affiliate marketing programs with Amazon Associates, Apple, Kobo (Rakuten), Barnes & Noble, and more.

Yes, it requires a lot of upfront work to set up affiliate accounts, but you only have to do it once and benefit from it indefinitely. Start with the platforms where you are confident you'll sell books (i.e., Amazon). It's 100% okay and Amazon even encourages you to double dip earnings through their affiliate program. I would've never known about the Amazon Associates program had it not been for Amazon Author Central sharing it as an additional stream of revenue as an author.

To better track your results, get specific about which links you share and where. For example, during a sponsorship campaign a few years ago, I created a unique URL for each video to measure performance individually. Keep in mind, view count doesn't equal sales or email signups. Breaking your links into content-specific segments helps pinpoint exactly where traffic is coming from. That way, you can adjust your strategy based on what's working and double down on winning ideas.

For video-based calls-to-action, check your link performance within the first week to see how well it's performing. Don't lose heart if you're not getting immediate results. I've published quite a few sleeper videos over the years, some that still pay me affiliate earnings to this day. Give it time and a little patience. The results will come if you don't give up and you continue to improve and iterate on how you're sharing your CTA.

One last tool that'll prove helpful is the QR code. Readers can scan a QR code that redirects them to your product (be it a book, email list, or affiliate offer). You can insert a QR code on screen in your video or in your print books. Can QR code work in an ebook or audiobook? Yes, but I don't know how effective the conversion is for them. For ebooks, we could theorize that someone using an ereader could easily scan the QR code with their phone. Whereas with audiobooks, you'll probably want to include a downloadable PDF with your book containing the QR code.

With a QR code, you're better able to share your link. Then it's up to you to track all activity coming through a specific link. If you stick to it, eventually, you'll be able to know precisely where your efforts yield the best results (i.e., sell more books, get more email subscribers, etc.).

For now, if you take any one piece of advice and implement it today, I'd recommend tackling universal book links. Your readers will thank you!

CHAPTER 7:
MONETIZING YOUR CHANNEL WITHOUT SELLING OUT

A round 2017, a fellow video creator chatted with me about the YouTube Partner Program. He'd shared how the revenue was a nice little bonus for all his work. The conversation eventually leads to how much I was making, and the truth was I didn't have the ads turned on. My first channel was already well-established and qualified for the program, but I was quietly sitting on that part of my business.

Back then, the program was relatively easy to break into, so all I needed to do was fill out all the forms for Google AdSense, then turn ads on for all my videos. Within weeks, I saw a steady flow of earnings coming in (around $100 per month). Those earnings have grown significantly since then with a few dips and spikes here and there.

These days, it's much harder to qualify for the YouTube Partner Program. It's a whole different ball game that requires a ton of persistence and plenty of experimentation.

To qualify for the top tier option for the YouTube Partner Program, you'll need 1,000 subscribers and 4,000 watch time hours within a rolling year. There are other ways to break into the program, but this is the one I've used every time to get monetized.

HOW TO QUALIFY FOR THE YOUTUBE PARTNER PROGRAM (FASTER THAN YOU THINK)

My first channel got into the YouTube Partner Program just before major changes rolled out in early 2018. Since I had already met the new requirements, I wasn't affected. However, many of my friends and peers lost access and had to hustle to regain eligibility under the updated rules.

The second channel I monetized was my podcast. Here's how I hit the requirements within a year:

1. **I went live every week**. Consistent content helped build steady watch time.
2. **I focused on what authors cared about most**. This kept the content relevant and engaging.
3. **I created video series designed for binge-watching**. Authors could easily watch multiple episodes back-to-back, boosting retention and views.

Side note: When you share your video, don't just use the share option on the video's page. Instead, open your video from within a playlist. Then grab the long, ugly URL from the browser's address bar. When you share your video, use that link on YouTube. If you're sharing it elsewhere, it might be a good idea to shorten the link. You can use Pretty Links to shorten it.

Qualifying for the YouTube Partner Program might seem like a big leap, but it becomes much easier when you break it down into manageable steps:

1. **Be consistent**. Showing up every week builds trust and momentum. Don't fall into the trap of thinking quantity beats quality. One solid video is more valuable than ten forgettable ones.
2. **Focus on improvement**. Ask for feedback and be open to constructive criticism. Every video is a chance to get better.
3. **Be intentional**. Don't upload content without a plan. Apply what you've learned so far, and you'll be well on your way. When I'm trying to grow a channel, I always ask viewers to subscribe—and I tell them exactly what they'll gain by doing so.

If you want to qualify for the YouTube Partner Program, then your primary mission should be to get people to watch longer and subscribe. This means you might have to put your book promotion on-hold or be especially clever with how you incorporate a CTA to buy your book and subscribe to your channel.

Will having two calls to action hurt your video? Not necessarily, but focusing on just one makes it crystal clear what you want viewers to do. A single, focused CTA increases the chances they'll take meaningful action.

You've got several powerful content formats to choose from on YouTube. Here are the four main types to consider:

1. **Long-form video**: Traditional 16:9 format, ideal for tutorials, deep dives, or storytelling.

2. **Shorts**: Vertical videos up to 3 minutes long. Great for rapid growth and attracting new subscribers. Deliver value fast, then ask for the sub at the end.
3. **Livestreams**: Go live, interact in real time, and build trust. It's especially effective once you have an engaged audience.
4. **Community Posts**: A highly underrated tool. Use the **Posts** tab to stay top of mind and grow your community between uploads.

Try all four options in some capacity. The only way to truly know what resonates with you and your ideal audience is through a little trial and error. For authors that are lacking time, look into livestreaming and Shorts videos. Those two options require less work and can yield the same results if you're calculated with the type of content you're producing.

YOUTUBE AD REVENUE (THE BASICS)

Before you can monetize your videos, you'll need to be officially accepted into the YouTube Partner Program. After hitting the required subscriber and watch hour thresholds, you won't get immediate access. YouTube first reviews your channel, which usually takes a few days or more. Once approved, you'll receive an email notification letting you know it's time to complete the final setup steps.

One of those steps includes linking an active AdSense account. If you haven't set one up yet, take care of it early to avoid delays. The approval process for AdSense can take time, and you won't be able to fully monetize your channel without it.

Once you qualify and get acceptance into the YouTube Partner Program, it's time to turn on ads for the videos. But you need to be careful about loading up too many ads at first, especially based on the content you produce. For instance, if you were producing read-along videos where you're providing a relaxed atmosphere for the viewer, it probably makes no sense to use mid-roll ads. Don't worry, you'll still earn money from the pre- and post-roll ads.

Or, if you're working with a sponsor or pushing a product of your own, turn off ads for that given video. You can imagine how embarrassing it would be if you were promoting one brand, but the competing brand advertises over your video.

I recommend enabling ads on all your videos and including the mid-rolls if it makes sense for your content. You can turn on mid-roll ads for every video and can allow YouTube to place them automatically or you can handle it in the **Editor** feature in YouTube Studio.

While you can place many mid-roll ads on a video, that doesn't guarantee an ad will run every time for all viewers. YouTube's ad platform tries to present ads based on timing, demand, and interest. One viewer might see all of your mid-roll ads, while another viewer may not see a single ad.

For that reason, I do not recommend relying solely on YouTube ad revenue as a source of income. Consider it a bonus on top of your work and never rely on it performing a certain way every month. I've had some fantastic months that I wish lasted forever and other times that made me even wonder if the Partner Program was worth it.

Realistically, your earnings potential is going to vary wildly based on the content you produce and the audience you serve. Advertisers pay depending on the demand and you have no real say over the outcome. You could make hundreds or thousands per month, or little to nothing at all. You won't truly know until you get there.

In the meantime, focus on qualifying for the YouTube Partner Program while also diversifying your income. Explore options like book sales, courses, consultations, premium memberships, affiliate marketing, sponsorships, and more. These revenue streams often deliver faster results, and none of them require approval to get started.

AFFILIATE MARKETING FOR AUTHORS

Affiliate marketing is where you earn commissions for referring paying customers to a brand, service, or product. Finding these programs is dead simple. Consider your audience and what they currently use or relate to. Then, do a quick online search of the brand name plus "affiliate program" and you should get an easy access point.

Before I ever turned on ads for my videos, I earned money through affiliate marketing programs. Right around the time I scaled my video output and doubled down on YouTube, I'd leaned on affiliate marketing to bring in a consistent flow of revenue.

My first success with affiliate marketing came from Grammarly, the grammar-checking tool. I was already a fan of the product, so creating a review came naturally. I recorded for just a few minutes, wrapped it up in a couple of hours, and hit publish.

Although the video didn't perform well at first, momentum picked up in the weeks that followed, and YouTube began recommending it more often. I eventually removed it from public view after my opinions changed. Before I retired it, the video brought in:

- Nearly 100,000 views
- 3,400 watch time hours
- 496 new subscribers
- $1,036.49 in ad revenue

Not to mention, I'd made numerous affiliate sales because of the video, somewhere around the thousands. The short time investment paid off big time for me and this video seeded out many more ideas on how I could better leverage YouTube without the need of the Partner Program.

I learned the hard way that just because a product has an affiliate program doesn't mean it deserves a video. Since my content focuses on authors, I figured reviews of ereaders and tablets might be helpful. My thinking was that authors could use recommendations for their readers, so why not offer a resource?

There was one slight problem. The videos took off in a big way, but I started noticing an alarming number of people unsubscribing to my videos about writing and self-publishing. Believing that I was producing worse videos, I'd continue scratching my head for months, never giving the content a second thought.

Then it occurred to me. Even though I was producing videos for authors, YouTube perceived the content as for readers or anyone interested in ereaders or tablets. When I launched a video that had nothing to do with those two items, the reader-focused viewers unsubscribed.

While the revenue was nice from the Amazon Associates Program (their affiliate program), it wasn't enough to offset the damage it took on my channel. Thankfully, when I delisted the offending videos, my ad revenue dropped only a slight bit. I made up the difference in affiliate earnings through other programs and products relevant to my audience.

It's okay to experiment. Some results may surprise you. As long as you stay focused on your audience's needs and your channel keeps growing, even slowly, you're moving in the right direction.

The biggest piece of advice for affiliate marketing is to always disclose the nature of your arrangement with a company. I made it a habit to always state clearly in the video that it's an affiliate link and further share it in my video description. You'll also see an option in the upload process for disclosing paid promotions. Click on the "Show more" option and Paid promotion is right below that. The bottom line is: if you will receive or have received compensation for a video, you must check that box.

Viewers will see the disclosure statement at the beginning of the video, and it really doesn't seem to be detrimental to views. I've done many videos with affiliate links and sponsorships and have never seen a huge drop-off selecting that option. Don't be afraid to offer full transparency to your audience, it builds deeper trust.

SPONSORSHIPS THAT MAKE SENSE

I love sponsorships, they're like affiliate marketing on steroids. I think affiliate marketing is pretty incredible on its own, but with sponsorship revenue thrown into the mix, it creates a whole new dynamic for your earnings potential.

Brands and companies are always looking for new ways to reach their ideal audience. While many rely on paid ads through YouTube, that approach can get expensive, especially without a clear strategy. That's why some are willing to pay a premium to partner with creators who already have access to the audience they want.

That's where you come in. Regardless of your audience size, sponsorships are ready and waiting for you. Yes, it's going to be tougher landing a sponsorship deal when you have a small following or a modest backlist of videos. Stockpile enough of both items, then brands will be more eager to chat with you.

You'll want to have a few best practices in place before looking into sponsorships. Your YouTube channel needs to be fully set up with a professional profile image and channel banner. Consider loading up your channel with a dozen or more videos so that brands have undeniable proof that you know how to handle yourself on camera and have the chops to put together a good video.

Companies are less likely to trust unproven video creators with no experience, so make it more enticing for them. While you're building a backlog of videos, consider implementing at least two to three videos with an affiliate marketing plug. You can share an affiliate product through a demonstration, review, or listicle (i.e., top five, top ten), then push those videos to the moon. Track your results and store them away to share with potential sponsors.

What most sponsors want to know comes down to three things:

1. Can you produce high-quality videos?
2. Can you influence purchases through your content?
3. Will working with you deliver a positive return, either through brand exposure or direct sales?

Don't worry about trying to impress a brand with your follower count or average views. Share what you can do for the brand, keep it honest, and provide data from your previous success with affiliate marketing.

Now, if you're still reluctant about getting a sponsorship deal until you hit a specific subscriber milestone, I'd say make it 1,000. With less than 3,000 subscribers, I had a channel that pulled in regular sponsorship deals for about $2,500 per month. You just need to find the perfect crossroads of what your audience wants and what the brand needs.

Pitching a brand isn't complicated, but it can be tough if you're reaching out without an existing connection. I've mostly avoided cold outreach by building relationships through networking, which has led to the sponsorship deals I've wanted.

Some of the brands I've pitched through existing relationships include Draft2Digital, Dibbly Create, Book Award Pro, Miblart, GetCovers, and ProWritingAid. Since I already knew and used their services, asking for a sponsorship felt natural and straightforward.

First, I contact someone within the company that manages influencer marketing, brand deals, and sponsorships. Usually someone within marketing can help point me in the right direction. Next, I will book a video chat to discuss an exciting idea I have for a partnership. When we connect, I'm not looking to close them right away. All I want to know is what they expect and what kind of budget they're dealing with.

Most companies want to see direct sales, but not all sponsorships are conversion-based. You'll typically find three types:

1. **Conversion**: The brand expects your video to generate measurable sales.
2. **Awareness**: The goal is simply to increase visibility and brand recognition.
3. **Repurposing**: The company hires you to create content they can reuse on their own platforms.

Most of my sponsorship campaigns have focused on conversions, with only a few falling into the other categories.

A QUICK WORD OF WARNING ABOUT SCAMS

Be cautious of "growth network" scams or so-called YouTube partnership teams promising you instant access to high-paying sponsors, faster growth, or exclusive resources. These groups often ask for a cut of your revenue, require you to sign restrictive contracts, and offer little real value in return. If anyone cold emails or DMs you about joining a network that seems too good to be true, it probably is.

Always read contracts carefully. And if you're unsure, ask a trusted creator or attorney to review the terms before signing anything. Your content is your business. Protect it. Let's look at how to make that business relationship airtight.

No matter the sponsorship arrangement, always get the agreement in writing. Most companies have boilerplate contracts, but you can also bring your own. I strongly recommend having an attorney review any contract before signing, it can save you a lot of grief later.

Key contract terms to watch for:

1. **Perpetual license**: Never give a brand unlimited rights to your likeness or content. If you provide a video asset, set a clear expiration date. You can always negotiate a new deal later, but don't give away your future earnings potential.
2. **Non-compete clause**: Some brands are relaxed about this, while others use vague language like "don't work with our competitors." That can include almost anyone. Ask for a specific list of competitors to avoid confusion.
3. **Unlimited revisions**: Don't agree to it. Give the brand time to approve the concept, but once you begin production, limit how many revisions they can request. Also, include a deadline for when feedback must be submitted.
4. **Force majeure**: This clause protects both parties in case of emergencies. Be clear about how responsibilities shift if something unexpected happens, so there's no confusion during a worst-case scenario.
5. **Opt-out clause**: I allow sponsors to back out of a campaign, but they must pay for any completed work. Make sure this clause applies to both parties so you can walk away if a brand faces a PR crisis or reputational risk.

Once your attorney has reviewed the contract, you're ready to accept payment and begin the project. Never record a single frame until you've received at least a 50% deposit. I often tell clients, "I'm like McDonald's: you pay first, then I get to work." It's entirely up to you how you structure your payments, but make sure it protects your time and effort.

CHAPTER 7: MONETIZING YOUR CHANNEL WITHOUT SELLING OUT

Yes, pricing takes some guesswork in the beginning. When I started with sponsorships, I charged just $50 per video. Today, I charge $1,000 or more, but that growth came from experience, consistent results, and gradually scaling my rates as I proved I could deliver a strong return on investment for my sponsors.

What you create for sponsors is entirely up to you and your creativity. Just make sure the brand aligns with your audience and overall message. There are several effective ways to feature a product:

- **Product placement**: Subtly display the brand's product during your video.
- **Product demonstration**: Show how it works in action.
- **Product review**: Share your honest experience using the product.
- **Product comparison**: Stack it against similar tools or services.
- **Mid-roll ad**: Deliver a brief, scripted ad during your video content.

Most of the options I've mentioned involve creating content centered around the product, which means more work for you. If time is limited or a brand has a smaller budget, consider offering a mid-roll ad. Instead of letting YouTube insert ads, you create your own. Drop a short, engaging commercial into your video, just make it seamless. As I mentioned earlier, Ten Hundred does this brilliantly, blending sponsored content into his videos without disrupting the flow. Creators like MrBeast, Bobby Duke Arts, and Ryan George have also mastered the art of mid-roll delivery.

Some sponsors may want more than just a quick shoutout or a mid-roll ad. In those cases, you can co-develop content together. For example, I partnered with Fiverr to produce an entire YouTube series called *Book Rescue*, where the brand's services were baked into the format of each episode. This kind of collaboration goes beyond basic product placement. It creates something unique, valuable, and binge-worthy that serves both your audience and the brand. Just make sure the partnership aligns with your message and delivers real value to your viewers. When it's done right, these collaborations can become some of your most successful and satisfying projects.

Research your niche to see how others are producing their content with sponsors. Take notes and inspiration from every creator you watch and make it your own. Do you want to impress a brand? Show them one of the best mid-roll ads ever, an extraordinary video that encapsulates it, and you've got a sponsor for life.

While a sponsorship campaign runs, I'm keeping strict track of all metrics from the views and average watch time to affiliate link clicks and conversions. I like to check in with a brand at least once to twice per month, but most importantly, at the end of the campaign. If I know it went well, I immediately put together a proposal for the next campaign. I've already got great ideas lined up and ready so that we can transition from one campaign to the next seamlessly.

I highly recommend if you want a deeper understanding of how to land sponsorships, follow my good friend and fellow YouTuber, Justin Moore. Also known as Creator Wizard on social media, Justin is the brand deal whisperer. Catch his videos for a firm grasp on sponsorships and if you're really feeling bold, pick up a copy of his book *Sponsor Magnet*. It's a fantastic read and is chock full of actionable advice. Should you not feel like reading any of it, skip to the scripts he provides for landing a deal based on your situation. They're priceless!

If your channel is focused on fiction or reader-facing content, you are not excluded from sponsorships. In fact, reader-centric channels can appeal to a wide range of potential partners, including book subscription boxes, local bookstores, and lifestyle products like tea, candles, or home pampering kits. The key is alignment. If the product fits your brand and resonates with your audience, it is worth considering. A cozy fantasy channel might partner with a journaling brand. A sci-fi read-along series could highlight a tablet or ereader. Think about what your viewers would love, and then look for a brand that offers it.

MEMBERSHIPS AND EXCLUSIVE CONTENT

When you deliver enough value to your audience, they'll eventually want more from you and many will look for ways to give back directly.

Enter memberships.

Once you qualify for the base level of the YouTube Partner Program, you'll have the option to enable Channel Memberships. When it becomes available, turn it on and offer a simple entry-level tier focused solely on supporting your channel. Many viewers genuinely enjoy helping creators and are happy to contribute a few dollars just to show their support.

Even if you have nothing special to offer, just put something in place. That way, when someone is interested in supporting you, you're not floundering about or scrambling to put together an offer. Start with $1 to $5 with a special note that this is strictly to help support the channel. In return, you can provide all channel members with exclusive membership badges, emojis, and early access to future videos.

YouTube splits membership revenue 70/30, in your favor. Sadly, that might not sit well with quite a few of you, so if you're looking for other opportunities to start a membership that doesn't take as much a cut of the revenue, consider Patreon. I have little to no experience with Patreon, however, I've heard nothing but high praises for the platform.

My biggest reservation with using Patreon is that I'm driving people away from my YouTube channel, therefore, I'm going to lose some momentum. If I have channel members watching exclusive content, they're more apt to continue watching my other videos since YouTube is a central location.

When you're ready to scale up your offerings, I want you to consider what you could deliver to your members without creating a bunch of busy work. For me, I like to livestream for members only, review products, and show behind-the-scenes footage of my workflow and tools.

You'll know what's a hit or a dud when you have a few tiers available. Ask your audience through polls on your **Posts** Tab or during livestreams what they would expect out of each membership tier and how much it would cost. Your audience will be happy to guide you in the right direction.

When promoting your membership, the key is to avoid alienating your audience. Not everyone has money to spare, but many will still support you by watching your videos. Reassure viewers that membership is never expected, always appreciated. Yes, members will get extra perks, but they're paying for that added access. Ultimately, do what's best for your business. If someone chooses to support you, that's fantastic. If they don't, that's perfectly fine too.

Just like your calls to action, keep mentions of memberships or Patreon to a minimum within each video. Bring them up when it feels natural, especially after receiving strong support or enthusiastic feedback from your community. When you've built a loyal audience, that's the right time to introduce membership options.

Remember, promotion isn't limited to your videos. You can highlight your membership in your descriptions, email newsletter, website, or social media posts. But if you're deciding where to focus first, prioritize gaining subscribers and growing your email list. Once someone's inside your ecosystem, you can nurture that relationship and introduce the membership opportunity later.

Above all else, watch time still reigns supreme on YouTube. Whether someone joins your membership or not, keeping them engaged is what drives long-term success. So give yourself every advantage. Set up a simple membership option today and start turning your community into another meaningful income stream.

CHAPTER 8:
OPTIMIZING YOUR CHANNEL FOR GROWTH & DISCOVERABILITY

Back in 2017, I made a major pivot that reshaped everything: my mindset, my content, and my branding. To stand out in the crowded world of self-publishing channels, I knew I had to do things differently. That didn't mean reinventing the wheel. I just needed to look more professional and deliver more polished content. The polish came with time, but improving the visual presentation was quick. A few graphic updates and some channel setting tweaks went a long way.

Once I had my setup dialed in, the purpose of my channel became clear to anyone who visited. But that clarity didn't come from a one-time decision. I've continued to refine, test, and improve how I present my channel and how viewers discover it.

CUSTOMIZING YOUR CHANNEL LAYOUT FOR FIRST IMPRESSIONS

I cannot overstate the importance of using **YouTube Studio** to not only upload videos, but to track data, communicate with your viewers, and tweak your backend settings for better long-term results.

Although we briefly touched on channel customization, let's break into it a little further to increase the odds of discoverability and make a best first impression.

Access **YouTube Studio**, then select the **Customization** option in the left menu. Under the **Profile** tab, you'll need to fill in:

1. Banner image
2. Picture
3. Name
4. Handle
5. Description

The banner image is what viewers will see above your profile picture when they visit your channel's main landing page. You'll want to make the graphics:

1. 2048 x 1152 pixels
2. No larger than 6 megabytes
3. Important elements placed in the middle
4. Add context for what to expect in your videos

I design most of my graphics in GIMP, but even after years of using it, I'm still not that fast or polished. That's why I hand off my more important projects to Flocksy. Their designer consistently delivers higher-quality results than I could on my own.

You can look into other graphic design software or services like Photoshop, PhotoPea, Canva, or even Book Brush. These tools are all fantastic if you have the time and patience to learn them. With Canva, you already have templates for YouTube graphics, so all you'd have to do is tweak and adjust the layout and theme to make it your own.

Tell people what to expect in your banner. Some video creators are brave enough to put a video launch schedule in their banner, but I don't think that's how I want to run my business. I'd rather produce quality videos without the rush of a schedule. Publishing videos on YouTube shouldn't be strictly about a specific time. If you find a schedule helpful in keeping you on track, go for it. Wait to announce your schedule publicly until you're absolutely certain you can stick with it long term, with no exceptions.

Your channel banner should clearly tell viewers what to expect from your content. I've gone through several versions of mine and often use that space to promote my latest book. One of my most effective taglines was:

Publish books that sell.

It's entirely up to you to decide what you put in here. Once you upload the graphic and click **Publish**, check how it looks on desktop, mobile, and television. Are all the elements centrally located and easily visible? If not, adjust your graphics, then try again. This might take a few attempts but can be worth it. Think of the channel banner as a welcome mat leading into your house. You want viewers to know instantly what to expect when they watch one of your videos.

For the profile picture, I'll make this dead simple for you: it's you! Yes, you are the main character, our fearless protagonist, and now is the time for you to take center stage. A professional headshot would be ideal, but if you can't swing that, a simple picture with your smartphone will do. Just make sure you're placed in front of a neutral background with ample lighting.

You'll need your profile image to be:

- At least 98 x 98 pixels
- Less than 4MB
- Formatted as PNG or GIF (no animations)

Once you've chosen a strong profile picture, use it across all platforms, not just YouTube. Make sure your face fills about two-thirds of the image, keeping in mind that YouTube will crop it into a circle.

If you don't want your face in your profile picture, choose something memorable and easily recognizable. Avoid small or unreadable text. People will see this profile image anytime you post a video or comment, so make it a memorable picture that's easy to understand when shrunk down to a small thumbnail.

Don't waste your time with putting your book cover in the profile picture; it's simply too busy for anyone to discern any of the finer elements you've put into crafting a great cover. For profile pictures, less is more.

Also, stay consistent with it, that way people can identify your brand within a millisecond of viewing your profile pic.

Next, fill out your channel name. I recommend leading with your own name to help viewers remember you long after they've watched a video. When I first launched my channel, it was called *Self-Publishing with Dale L. Roberts*. The goal was clear—attract people interested in self-publishing—but the name was long and not easy to remember.

Fortunately, "Dale" isn't exactly common, so I shortened it to *Self-Publishing with Dale*, which was simpler and more memorable.

As I mentioned earlier, I split my focus between two YouTube channels, which eventually called for distinct branding. I kept the podcast channel named *The Self-Publishing with Dale Podcast*, while I rebranded the main channel under my full name, *Dale L. Roberts*. Using my name made it easier for viewers to remember me when searching for books or videos about self-publishing. After all, I've made a point to feature my name consistently across all platforms.

The next option is to reserve a handle. Choose something that involves your author name with no deviation. If you find it's taken already, try using additional words like "author" or "the." Don't settle for the first thing that comes to you because this is something that'll help you later drive traffic to the right YouTube channel.

Once you have a handle reserved, click **Publish** to save it.

To access your YouTube channel, you can tell people to search for your handle or visit YouTube.com/@(your handle here). For example, my YouTube channels are at:

- Dale L. Roberts: YouTube.com/@DaleLRoberts
- The Self-Publishing with Dale Podcast: YouTube.com/@SelfPubWithDale

Next, fill out your channel description. Start with a strong hook that tells viewers exactly what they can expect. You don't need to explain every detail about yourself, most people won't read the entire thing. I use this space to clarify my channel's purpose and include relevant keywords to boost search visibility in my niche.

Avoid stuffing your description with links or over-the-top self-promotion. Your goal is to hook viewers, not pitch to them. Focus on getting them to watch your videos. That's how you boost watch time, improve discoverability, and increase product sales over the long term.

The next section is for links, but use them sparingly. Ask yourself: what's your main goal on YouTube? If you're focused on growing your channel and qualifying for the Partner Program, your top priority should be a subscribe link, nothing else.

Here's a little trick you can use for a link that auto-subscribes a viewer. At the end of the URL to your YouTube channel, insert *?sub_confirmation=1* after it. For instance, if I wanted someone to subscribe to my channel, this link will prompt them to subscribe:

https://www.youtube.com/@dalelroberts?sub_confirmation=1

You get bonus points if you use a Pretty Link or custom domain. Any time I want someone to subscribe to my channel, I don't rattle off all that mess above; I use DaleLinks.com/YouTube.

If you're not focused on growing your YouTube channel and just want to sell more books, then this section should point viewers where you want them to go. Start with the most important link. I recommend using a free tool like *Linktree*, which gives you a landing page to organize everything in one place. You can add clickable icons for social media, plus direct links to your books, newsletter, and website.

Linktree tracks click activity, so you can see which links get the most engagement and deserve more attention. While tools like this are helpful, they're optional. You can always build a custom landing page on your own website. I've found *Linktree's* free tier to be surprisingly effective.

Just like your profile image, use your catch-all link consistently across platforms so people always know where to learn more about you and your brand.

The next step in customizing your channel is adding an email address for business inquiries. Never share the one you use to log into YouTube. That's a gift to hackers. Instead, use a separate business email that isn't tied to your login.

I've received plenty of brand deals, sponsorships, and freebies just from having this information filled out. When someone visits your main channel page and clicks the "...more" option, they'll see your description, links, and under **More info**, the option to **View email address**. YouTube hides the email behind a clickable button, likely to prevent scammers or bots from scraping it easily.

The last item to set is your **video watermark**. This digital stamp appears in the bottom-right corner of every video, and you can choose when it displays:

- End of the video
- Custom start time
- Entire video

Clicking this icon gives viewers the option to subscribe, but don't put too much weight on it, most people don't even notice it. If you do use a watermark, make sure it's a square image with a transparent background, saved as a PNG file.

Once you're done filling out the **Profile**, click the **Publish** and **View channel** buttons. Make sure everything looks good, then return to your dashboard and visit the **Home** tab.

This will be all the content below your channel information, usually appearing as content carousels. The first options are for videos that welcome new viewers and acknowledge returning viewers. For your channel trailer, shoot a short one-minute video of who you are and what your channel is about. It doesn't have to be perfect, just get it done, and upload it. Truthfully, a channel trailer is only a placeholder.

When you find a video that performs well in views and brings in new subscribers, use it as your welcome video. If it already convinced people to subscribe, it's likely to attract even more first-time viewers to your channel.

Give it time, because finding the right video to feature might take a few tries. You'll also need to update it occasionally as your goals shift. In the **Featured video for returning subscribers** section, choose the video you want to gain more traction. This should be your hero video, the one you pour the most time, energy, and attention into. You'll probably change it more often than your welcome video, depending on your current focus.

The following sections are what you fill out as you grow your channel. You'll want to have as a minimum in your allotted channel sections:

- **For You**: YouTube is more likely to know what videos your potential viewer wants to watch based on watch history. Give them the steering wheel here.
- **Videos**: Use this list to display your latest videos. This gives viewers a sense of the frequency and recency of videos you

published. A dead or dormant channel can turn off potential viewers, deeming the content as outdated or irrelevant.
- **Single playlist**: Load up all your video series into separate sections. Lead with the playlist with the most views, then add in more as you go.

You can add more sections based on what interests you most. I like to showcase other channels similar to mine or have some relation to me personally. You can find that in the **Featured channels** section.

Fill up every slot once you have enough content. Once you're in the Partner Program, you can also display your merchandise (via Shopify, Spring, or Spreadshirt). You can also add a **Member recognition** section to spotlight randomly selected members (a minimum of eight members required).

Once you're ready, click the **Publish** and **View Channel** buttons in the top right corner. Take your time reviewing how your channel looks on both desktop and mobile. Make any adjustments you need, then let your channel do the work of attracting your ideal viewer.

CHANNEL SETTINGS THAT SUPPORT GROWTH

We've reached the final section for fine-tuning your channel to boost discoverability and efficiency. The good news? You've already started this process by setting default upload details like the description.

Go to **Settings** in the bottom-left corner of YouTube Studio (on desktop), and you'll see several useful options:

- **General**: Choose the currency displayed in your revenue dashboard.

- **Channel**: Set up your basic info, advanced settings, and feature eligibility.
- **Upload defaults**: Add default titles, descriptions, tags, and monetization settings.
- **Ad categories**: Block specific URLs or ad categories from appearing on your channel. This is especially important if you have sponsors and want to suppress competitor ads.
- **Permissions**: Assign channel roles to trusted collaborators. Never give full ownership access unless you're transferring or selling your channel.
- **Community moderation**: Set filters, comment defaults, and your channel's community guidelines.
- **Creator demographics**: Optional info that mainly helps YouTube. Fill it out if you like.
- **Agreements**: View all digital contracts you've accepted within the platform.

To keep things simple, let's focus on three key sections: **Channel**, **Upload defaults**, and **Community moderation**.

To improve your channel's discoverability, go to the **Channel** tab and open **Basic info**. There, you can enter up to 500 characters of relevant keywords that describe your content. Not sure what to include? Use an AI tool to help brainstorm keyword ideas that align with your niche.

You should have a firm grasp on common keywords for your niche, so fill this in and remember, you can always come back later to adjust these keywords.

Under **Advanced settings** in the **Channel** tab, you'll find the audience settings. Unless your videos are specifically made for children, select **No, set this channel as not made for kids.**

This won't stop kids from watching your videos—it simply tells YouTube that your content is intended for a general audience. It doesn't mean you're using profanity or mature themes; it just ensures YouTube classifies and handles your videos appropriately.

Around 2019, YouTube forced all video creators serving content for children to disclose it upon publishing. Creators who were publishing kid's videos lost quite a few privileges, including limited ads and no comments. If I haven't made it clear enough yet: you need comments to build a strong community on YouTube. Unless you're publishing videos specifically geared towards kids, always label your videos as not made for children.

In the **Upload defaults** tab, you should already have that filled out with the relevant links and details about your author brand and include an affiliate disclosure for safe measure. I set my videos as Unlisted when uploading so I don't make the mistake of publishing a video that's not ready for the public (i.e., waiting for approval from a sponsor). When I want to share the unpublished video, I can grab the link and give it to whoever I want. As long as someone has the link, they can view the video. It's a sweet feature if you're wanting to give early access to Patreon members but aren't in the YouTube Partner Program yet.

The final section worth your attention is **Automated filters** under **Community moderation**. Here, you can add channel URLs for trusted users who can help moderate your live chat. They won't have access to your dashboard—only the ability to manage comments during livestreams (such as banning users, flagging messages, or removing spam). Only grant this access to people you truly know and trust.

Just below that, you'll find the **Hidden users** section. This is where you manage people you've blocked from commenting on your channel.

Scroll down to the **Blocked words** section. I've added every common expletive and known scam phrase to keep my comment section family-friendly. Over time, your list will grow, but the more proactive you are, the fewer toxic comments make it through.

One of the most important settings to enable is blocking links during live broadcasts. While most viewers have good intentions, a small number may spam your chat with unsafe or irrelevant links. I've avoided issues by trusting my moderators to share links responsibly during livestreams. If you're running the stream solo, review any link before approving it, or simply delete it and move on.

Take your time navigating and exploring the customization and settings tools within your dashboard. Every element plays a part—whether big or small—in the growth and long-term success on YouTube. When in doubt, ask an expert. I'll have a list of resources in the back of the book. A few video creator experts to consider include:

- Creator Insider
- YouTube Insider (Rene Ritchie)
- Derral Eves
- Nick Nimmin
- Brian G. Johnson
- Roberto Blake

The good news is once you pass 10,000 subscribers, you have direct support options from within your dashboard where you can get clearer answers. Usually, I can figure my way around things with content from the previously mentioned creators and have rarely needed to lean on support for either of my channels above 10,000 subscribers. You'll get to that milestone eventually, just don't give up.

CHAPTER 9:
ADVANCED STRATEGIES TO ACCELERATE CHANNEL GROWTH

B eyond publishing binge-worthy videos with compelling titles and enticing thumbnails, how do you get your channel up to that next level? Persistence will get you there eventually, but you can create binge-worthy video series, tap into a larger community resource, or produce content for a different audience subset from normal video content.

EXPANDING YOUR BRAND THROUGH PLAYLISTS AND VIDEO SERIES

The term "playlist" on YouTube refers to their organizational system for a video series. As we've already discussed at great length, YouTube loves when you keep a viewer's attention. They love it even more when you can keep that watch time going for well beyond the first video. When you get a viewer to continue watching repeatedly for longer periods, you're sending positive signals to YouTube's algorithm. In return, you get more recommendations, which lead to more viewers, subscribers, watch time, and overall growth.

Playlists are invaluable because they let you repurpose individual videos into a new piece of content. YouTube treats playlists like standalone videos, which means you're effectively doubling your reach. Every video you create should belong to a playlist. Focus on the overarching theme, and whenever you produce a similar video, add it to that same list.

Video series are a powerful way to connect related content into a cohesive, bingeable experience. Keep testing different themes and formats, and don't get discouraged if one doesn't take off right away. Growth comes from experimentation.

> *Side note: You can track playlist performance in* **YouTube Studio Analytics**. *Go to* **Content**, *then select* **Playlists** *to view your top five performing series, total views, and views generated from within playlists. For a deeper dive, click* **See more** *at the bottom to access additional tools and filters.*

Where do you put a video that doesn't fit anywhere? Create a catch-all playlist for your channel that is optimized for your niche. Something is better than nothing. You can always create another playlist in the future and re-organize that video.

Just as you plan a title or description for a video, you'll want to put the same effort into each playlist. Do your research, develop a keyword-rich title and description, and have AI assist if you ever get stumped. Of course, make the playlist available to the public.

I'll return to the advice I shared earlier: share video links from within a playlist. Sending someone to watch your video automatically cues them to the next video in the series. Eventually, YouTube will recommend additional videos in the series or from your channel.

People often ask how I reached 1,000 subscribers and 4,000 watch hours so quickly. The answer: playlists. Of course, my videos and livestreams helped, but what made the biggest impact was sharing links from within playlists. This kept viewers watching multiple videos, boosting my watch time significantly. Once you meet the minimum requirements for the YouTube Partner Program, you can ease off a bit. Until then, this strategy will take you far.

Some creators have wondered if they can game the system by playing their own playlists on repeat to boost watch time. While it might sound harmless, YouTube's algorithm is smarter than that. They actively detect artificial watch behavior, including patterns that suggest manipulation. If flagged, you could lose monetization or have your revenue withheld. In short, don't try to game the system. Focus on creating content that keeps real viewers coming back. That's what builds a channel worth watching and worth monetizing.

COLLABORATION FOR GROWTH

The rising tide truly does raise all the boats, but you have to be in the right harbor to reap the rewards. Although YouTube is a vast ecosystem with millions of creators, the algorithm makes sense of the chaos and does its best to serve the right option for the right viewer at the right time.

If you want to stretch the value of a single video, consider collaborating. Whether it's with another author or a brand, collaborations create a win-win-win: both parties gain exposure to each other's audiences, and viewers benefit from getting two trusted voices in one video.

Only collaborate if it makes sense. Unlike your previous solo ventures in video, you're now having to work in tandem with another creator. You might have to relinquish some creative control or compromise on production ideas. Is that a bad thing? No, but it can be if you choose the wrong person to collaborate with.

I've had my share of rough collaborations on YouTube, usually because I rushed into them. Just because you get along with someone once or twice doesn't mean you're ready to work together. Make sure there's a solid relationship in place before teaming up. Otherwise, things can get messy fast.

First, approach creators you actually want to work with. Don't simply choose someone based on their follower count; focus more on what they bring to the table. Having millions of followers doesn't change the fact that you still have to put in the same work with a video creator who has a small following. Set expectations before you break into a project and always discuss alternatives in case your video collaboration goes side ways.

Next, putting together a video should include input from both creators, but you will have to decide who is the chief content producer and where the video will reside. I recommend putting a video collaboration on either channel, not both. Otherwise, it defeats the purpose of doing a video collaboration: to cross-pollinate audiences. If you want a reciprocal setup, consider creating separate videos in your own styles or producing a two-part series, with the first video on the larger channel and the second on the smaller one.

The idea is simple: the first video introduces the smaller channel to a wider audience, making viewers more likely to watch the follow-up. When the second video launches, it combines the smaller channel's existing audience with the new viewers from the first video, giving the smaller creator a meaningful boost.

This cross-pollination is beneficial in many ways, including YouTube's recommended traffic. When a viewer watches enough overlap of videos from various content creators, they're more likely to be served videos like it. Collaboration is one way to train the algorithm that two creators share the same audience, therefore extending reach for everyone involved.

Last, be sure you have everything fine-tuned the way you both like it, and iron out a post-launch promotional plan for the video. It's not enough for you to publish a video; you both are now responsible for building awareness around it.

Hit up your email list and social media; post it on your website, blog, or forum. Leave no stone unturned. Ideally, you'll want to have a promotional post at least once per day over the first week, that way you can capitalize on any additional momentum from watch time and views.

What's the best way to contact someone about a collaboration? It comes down to timing and logic. Do you have the time to take on extra work beyond what you already do? If not, it's not the right time. Will a video collaboration make sense for both you and the proposed collaborator? I know it'd be sweet to partner with someone having millions of subscribers, but you run into an issue with audience interests. If your audiences share nothing in common, it probably makes little sense.

You're a writer, so I have no doubt you can find a creative way to make it work. Just don't feel like you have to do everything at once, especially if you're just getting started with YouTube. Focus on building a strong foundation first. Once you've published a dozen or more videos and feel more confident, collaborations can be a great next step. Take your time and grow at a pace that feels sustainable.

Once you've gained some traction, the best potential collaborators might already be in your YouTube Studio Analytics. Go to **Audience**, then scroll to **Channels your audience watches** and **What your audience watches**.

Bingo.

Not every channel will be a perfect fit, so take time to scout them. Watch their content and decide if a collaboration makes sense. If it does, reach out through their channel details. If no email is listed, check their video descriptions or social media links, you'll usually find a way to connect.

STRATEGIC PLAY WITH YOUTUBE SHORTS

Short form, vertical video content exploded in 2020 when TikTok became the talk of social media. Every platform was quick to copy them, and YouTube was among the first. While we could argue ethics over lifting an idea from another company, let's focus more on the positive impact YouTube Shorts has had on the platform.

In 2024, YouTube Shorts were viewed over 70 billion views per day.[iv] That's a massive audience you can tap into—especially if you're:

- Looking to create content more efficiently
- Wanting to grow your subscriber base
- Hoping to reach a different subset of viewers

Shorts cater to a different style of content consumption. Viewers crave fast, vertical content, and YouTube Shorts meet that demand perfectly.

CHAPTER 9: ADVANCED STRATEGIES TO ACCELERATE CHANNEL GROWTH

To qualify as a YouTube Short, your video must be:

- Vertical
- 3 minutes or less

Don't render your Short in a 16:9 aspect ratio, that's landscape (horizontal) format. Instead, use a 9:16 aspect ratio, which is vertical and fills the screen without black bars on the sides. YouTube will then automatically place your video on the Shorts Shelf, a vertical-scrolling carousel where viewers discover short-form content tailored to their interests.

You can meet certain qualifications for the YouTube Partner Program using Shorts, but it's been my experience that it's a steep hill to climb. I've had plenty of success with Shorts but would come nowhere near to qualifying for the Partner Program if I measured those views alone. They require millions of views, so you have to tap into trends or mainstream topics.

I view short-form video as a tool to attract new subscribers. Most of my content requires longer, more in-depth tutorials that simply don't fit into a three-minute format. Still, Shorts have proven effective. They've brought in new subscribers and generated ad revenue I wouldn't have earned otherwise. YouTube even offers bonus payments for Shorts, and it usually takes just a few minutes to create a one-minute video.

One way to repurpose your content is through the **Remix** feature on the YouTube mobile app. You'll need to enable your video for Shorts remixing by scrolling all the way to the bottom of your video's metadata. Under Shorts remixing, select **Allow video and audio remixing**. Yes, this gives permission to anyone who wants to reuse and share your video how they see fit. However, they still have to give you credit and it's also an indirect marketing opportunity, so let it play out.

To turn part of a long-form video into a Short, visit the video and tap the **Remix** button below it. You can trim a highlight down to under 60 seconds or even 15 seconds. As of 2025, you can't splice together multiple clips, and all edits must be done within the YouTube mobile app.

Once your Short is ready, publish it as **Unlisted**. Then go to YouTube Studio, find the video, and update the metadata. In the **Related video** section, link it to the original long-form video you clipped. This adds a clickable on-screen link that sends viewers directly to the full version. It's a simple way to drive traffic to your deeper content and boost overall watch time.

My biggest advice for YouTube Shorts is to keep it simple. The videos I spent hours perfecting often got less engagement than the raw, unpolished ones. That doesn't mean the successful ones were low quality, but they didn't match the level of polish I normally aim for. Remixes help preserve your message, though they don't always work when your content needs more context to land.

Give Shorts a shot. Many creators have found serious growth through short-form content. Just know the ad revenue will be lower than what you'd get from long-form videos or livestreams. That's because longer videos allow for more ad placements and higher watch time.

I treat YouTube Shorts as a tool for visibility, not direct income. They're a great way to reach new viewers and convert them into subscribers. Experiment, see what resonates, and when you find a winning idea, create more just like it. Build momentum one short video at a time.

CHAPTER 10:
SUSTAINING SUCCESS & PLANNING FOR LONG-TERM GROWTH

For over nine years, I've had my share of difficulties with the biggest complications coming around 2020. My main channel had exploded in popularity, and I was raking in more views and revenue than ever. Add to it, I was managing my weekly recordings on the podcast channel, plus trying to be an author.

Sadly, with all the success came all the stress. As my attention became split in too many directions, I found my personal time whittled down and my daily sleep schedule precariously balancing around four to five hours. The podcast channel was performing well, but not at the level of my larger channel. I was only one year into launching that secondary channel, so I wasn't disappointed having to halt work there so I could find a better work-life balance.

Don't fall into that trap! It's incredibly seductive to keep working harder than ever when you see massive results. The issue is you have to determine when enough is enough.

I'm not encouraging you to spread yourself too thin or to take on yet another project beyond your writing. It's a lot to ask, I know.

Then, accounting for the time to get real traction on YouTube, you might feel like it's a never-ending uphill battle.

When you feel that way, remember it's video content, not brain surgery; take a deep breath. No one's life is on the line, so don't take it too seriously. When you feel you're burned out, stressed, or anxious, take a step back and see where you can improve your approach, whether through mindset or workflow processes.

REVIEWING AND REFINING CONTENT STRATEGY OVER TIME

Even though I technically started on YouTube in April 2016, I never really put in the genuine work until June 2017. That was the first time when I re-analyzed my content and decided that it wasn't cutting it. Even though my thumbnails and video titles needed work, they weren't the main issue. It was the content. The videos were dull, uninspired, and the dialogue was all over the place.

I went back to the drawing board and executed a plan I still follow today:

1. **Research the niche**: Study successful creators and understand what viewers respond to.
2. **Identify trending keywords**: Use YouTube search, autosuggest, and free tools to find what people are searching for.
3. **Uncover pain points**: Read comments on videos in your niche to learn what viewers struggle with or want help on.
4. **Draft your assets**: Start with a clickable title and thumbnail, then create your outline or script.
5. **Shoot, edit, and publish**: Focus on clarity and value, then publish the video and track the results.

Up to that point, I'd only taken a shot in the dark at what some questions authors would have. Initially, I sourced my content ideas through questions I got in DMs on social media or email. Eventually, I exhausted my questions and had to guess.

Once I audited my content, my workflow, and my mindset, I got on right track with more clarity of purpose and razor-sharp focus. After that, I went on my daily video publishing spree until I had enough and slowed down my pace.

In a matter of four months, I had enough data and information to move forward with a better game plan. My videos became more polished and a little less scripted. I reinvested my YouTube earnings back into better equipment and video editing software. Slow but sure, my content improved.

All along the way, I regularly reviewed what I was doing and the results I was getting. Some videos would take off immediately, while others faded into obscurity. I used to take it personally when a video flopped, but I came to understand it wasn't a reflection of my worth. A video that doesn't engage viewers simply means I missed the mark—so I adjust and try again.

It's not the algorithm's fault. We create videos for people, not formulas. And while the algorithm isn't perfect, it generally does a good job of recommending content that keeps viewers watching.

Pay close attention to YouTube Studio Analytics in the first seven days of launching a video. Any channels with a substantial following (100 subscribers or more) get a little boost from pushing video notifications to their subscriber base. Once the subscribers interact with that video, YouTube gets to work on determining who else would enjoy this content.

For newer channels, it might take a month or more for a video to gain traction. Don't get discouraged—but also don't keep using the same strategy and expect different results. At some point, you'll publish a video that underperforms. When that happens, start by analyzing the following:

- **Title and thumbnail**: Are they compelling enough to earn clicks and keep viewers watching?
- **Audience retention chart**: In the Overview tab of your video analytics, scroll to the bottom to find this graph. A steady line is ideal. Sudden drops mean something in that moment caused viewers to leave or skip ahead. Click the dip to view that section of the video and pinpoint the issue.
- **Video performance ranking**: YouTube compares each new upload to your previous ten videos. A video that ranks #10 consistently signals a problem. But if you're seeing regular #1 rankings, your content is hitting the mark and your channel is moving in the right direction.

Side note: I know it's goofy to get this excited about a minor feature, but I'm sharing it anyway. Anytime a video ranks #1 out of the last ten uploads within the first twenty-four hours, YouTube gives you a little fireworks display on screen. I'm not gonna lie, I've refreshed the page a few times just to enjoy an extended victory celebration.

Do not be afraid to explore your YouTube Studio dashboard, and I even highly recommend downloading the YouTube Studio app (for iOS and Android). When I'm pressed for time and need quick answers, I lean on the app. I'm a stickler for checking my stats in the first twenty-four hours (see previous mention of fireworks) so I can adjust the title or thumbnail to get better results.

I rarely change the thumbnails anymore since I currently rely heavily on YouTube's three-way split test. When I need to cycle out those thumbnails, I simply grab the best of the original three and have it compared to two new iterations. Never give up on a video. If it's evergreen content, keep working on making it more discoverable and accessible to your ideal viewing audience.

Once you see a video take off, double down on that concept. Figure a way you can shoot another video that is a companion piece or sequel to the previous one. For instance, your successful video is *Top 10 Scariest Sci-fi Horror Books of 2025*, so you can always do other videos like it.

- *10 MORE of the Scariest Sci-fi Horror Books of 2025*
- *10 Hidden Sci-fi Horror Gems You Missed in 2025*
- *10 Upcoming Sci-fi Horror Books You Need on Your Radar (Late 2025–2026)*
- *Battle of the Titans: Best vs. Scariest Sci-fi Horror of 2025*
- *What Makes a Sci-fi Horror Book Truly Scary? (2025 Edition)*
- *Ranking the Best Sci-fi Horror Book Covers of 2025*

We could brainstorm dozens more ideas from this single video alone. When you discover a video takes off, don't just shrug your shoulders and chalk it up to luck. Figure out where you went right, then do it again.

To find the best days and times to publish, head to YouTube Studio's **Analytics**, then select the **Audience** tab. Once your channel has enough activity, you'll see a chart showing when your viewers are on YouTube. It displays the seven days of the week with twenty-four color-coded time slots each. The darker the shade, the fewer viewers are online. The brighter the shade, the more likely your audience is active.

Schedule your videos to go live at the start of a bright zone. For example, my analytics show:

1. **Sunday, Tuesday, and Friday**: Peak traffic hits between 10:00 a.m. and 1:00 p.m.
2. **Tuesday and Thursday**: Highest activity spans from 8:00 a.m. to 5:00 p.m.

Timing matters, but don't overthink it. Try out a few different time slots, see what performs best, and stick with what works. I've seen great results on my podcast channel by going live on Monday evenings, then trimming the second half of the show for a Tuesday upload. Over time, my live audience has grown, and the repurposed clips continue to do well.

AVOIDING BURNOUT AND STAYING MOTIVATED

Building a presence on YouTube takes time, patience, and a clear sense of purpose. It's easy to get caught up in views, subscriber counts, or monetization goals, but those numbers won't sustain your motivation.

Burnout is inevitable if you lose sight of why you're doing all of this. Don't come to YouTube expecting an audience to materialize and revenue to come pouring in. YouTube is a long-term play that'll set your platform up for compounding growth in the coming years. You just have to stick to it and never give up.

Take your time, experiment a little, and never allow yourself to resent YouTube. It'll all come together when you're ready and if you have to take a break or reanalyze your approach, do it. Your future self will thank you.

Don't pour your heart and soul into YouTube unless you're fully committed. Give yourself a break and some time away. Analyze and process why you're feeling burned out. It might not even be the videos. Maybe it's your workload or expectations.

To avoid burnout before it starts, draft a clear business plan for your YouTube channel. Define exactly what you want from the platform, not vague ideas like "become famous" or "get rich." Instead, focus on specific, measurable goals. For example: "I want to sell ten books per day" or "gain ten new subscribers daily." Once your target is set, reverse engineer your efforts so that every task and video supports that objective. Let your goal guide your strategy.

Once you've set your end goal, adjust your plan and aim for the next meaningful milestone. If you fall short, reflect on what went wrong. Repeated failure might mean you're taking on too much. Scale back your workload so you can experience small wins that keep you motivated.

When everything is running smoothly, I can usually build a backlog of one to two weeks' worth of content—about six videos or more.

Scheduling in advance lifts the pressure of staying consistent. YouTube thrives on fresh, engaging content, and the best way to keep the algorithm happy is to publish regularly. Keeping the platform fed with new videos allows me to focus on future projects and refine my older content.

Every creator faces burnout. The key is how you manage it. Sometimes, the best solution is to step away. Take a break for a week, a month, or even longer. The moment you begin to resent the process, it's time to regroup and find your balance again.

REINFORCING YOUR AUTHOR BRAND AS YOU GROW

The longer you work on YouTube, the more you'll discover your voice. But you can't simply do that by being passive. That means you need to be publishing videos at least once per month if you want to see any results. Weekly video upload schedules show you far more data over a year. Of course, you can double that output and get even more data.

Regardless of the frequency at which you publish videos, stick to it consistently. Settle into a schedule that you can manage without too much extra hassle. As time goes on, you'll get better at YouTube. Your confidence, presentation, video editing, and ideation will improve.

You will change and evolve as a person. It's okay to embrace that change, just remember to take your audience along for the ride and always be true to yourself. Viewers will always appreciate it, and it'll further cement your author brand on YouTube. Just keep being that go-to person in your niche.

This means you should change up your profile picture, channel banner, description, and the like. No one person stays the same forever and the same holds true for your author brand. Don't be afraid to take creative risks. Your viewers should be your co-pilot so that you don't have to navigate YouTube on your own.

Keeping your channel visually fresh is part of staying connected with your audience, but it's not just about looks, it's about continually raising the bar. Every time you show up, you have an opportunity to refine not only your brand but also your value in the eyes of your viewers.

Every time I produce a video, I try to make it better than any others in my niche. Why? Because I want to deliver the best and be the go-to person in all of self-publishing. Should I ever pivot to covering sci-fi horror books, that's what I'd want to dominate in.

Decide early how you want to be seen as an author, and let that vision guide you. Stay focused on that goal, and with enough grit and perseverance, you'll get there.

CONCLUSION: LIVING THE DREAM—FROM VHS TAPES TO GLOBAL REACH

Several years ago, I transferred a few old VHS home videos to digital and locked in those early memories for good. I looked awkward and goofy on camera, but I didn't care. I had no idea those casual recordings would lead to anything more than weekend fun with a friend. That hobby grew into something far bigger. Back then, the internet barely existed, and I had no way to imagine where this path would take me.

So much has changed since I was filming home videos, and not just the family's bulky VHS camcorder. Technology has come a long way. Today, we carry pocket-sized devices that would've seemed like science fiction back then. They're part TV, part computer, and fully connected to the internet, giving you instant access to anything you could ever want to see, learn, or share.

The good news is that if you're writing or publishing books, then you already understand the power of visibility and opportunity. Still, one of the biggest fears authors face is whether YouTube is just another shiny object. It's not, if you approach it with clear goals and a purpose that aligns with your author brand.

Authors today have a distinct advantage over those in the past, thanks to the wide array of tools available now. While the options can feel overwhelming, they also open the door to new ways of expanding your platform and diversifying your income. With YouTube's massive daily user base, you're never speaking into a void. And with the platform's steady growth year after year, starting now gives you the chance to build a lasting legacy for future generations to discover and enjoy.

YOU DON'T HAVE TO BE PERFECT

Before you ever sink a single solitary buck into building your YouTube channel, I want you to remind yourself that it doesn't have to be perfect. One great example of not being perfect while winning big is the story of my old friend, Walter Weyburn.

I first crossed paths with prolific indie author Walter Weyburn when he became active in my community. Any time I went live, Walter was there to cheer me on, ask questions, and interact with the other authors in the chat. Walter was one of the most lovable guys you could meet. He was a true throwback to a southern gentleman, though he could get fiery when he wanted.

Fast forward to early 2020 and Walter was going through some tough times. Amazon had deplatformed him years ago, but he continued to run a thriving and profitable book business with direct sales on his site. Sadly, traffic must've slowed down and sales came to a halt. Walter was beside himself, but I assured him that if he stuck to it, he'd come out smelling like roses.

Around April 2020, I checked in on Walter's YouTube channel and discovered it had taken off during the early days of lockdown. As I watched a few of his videos, something stood out. He used a low-quality webcam that barely hit 360p resolution, a basic USB microphone, and recorded everything in a single take. Walter would sit down, press record, talk, then publish. Despite the barebones setup, his lower-performing videos still brought in tens of thousands of views. His top videos? They were pulling in hundreds of thousands of views.

I contacted Walter to congratulate him on his success and, true to form, he gave me all the praise in the world.

Within a year, Walter earned the YouTube Silver Play Button for surpassing 100,000 subscribers. True to his generous nature, he did something completely unexpected. Shortly after reaching the milestone, he told me a package was on the way. A few weeks later, I opened it to find a Silver Play Button he had sent me. You can see my reaction on Instagram (link in the Resources).

He gave me full credit for his complete turnaround and considered me a vital part to him never giving up. Walter had tried YouTube so many times before. When he finally threw up his hands and surrendered to just being himself, people fell in love with him.

His good fortune continued for nearly a year until his passing. Every time I look at his Silver Play Button hanging on my wall, I'm reminded that it's okay to be imperfect. People will resonate with you as long as you show the world exactly who you are.

Growth on YouTube, like writing books, is a craft you'll improve with time. For now, be okay with your imperfections. Eventually, you'll get to where those old imperfections are gone, and you have new challenges and hills to climb. Till then, don't beat yourself up about being perfect.

START SHARING YOUR STORY NOW

Here we are, coming to the end of our little chat together. Before we part ways, I want to give you the next big steps and some final thoughts. Your first big mission is to lay the foundation of your presence on YouTube. Set up and optimize your channel right away.

Your next big action is to produce your first dozen videos. Take your time, but don't be so long that you stall out before the channel ever launches. When you feel confident you have your first few videos, publish them. Then schedule out your next several videos. Add more content regularly and analyze the data after launch.

YouTube is one of the greatest tools you have to reach readers, sell books, and build a lasting author brand. Show up consistently, and the platform will reward your effort. Keep going, and your results will compound year after year.

I have a final parting thought to consider as you boldly take a step into a new direction for your author business. It's not much, but it's enough to light your wick so you're motivated on even your worst day. Here it is:

You have a voice. You have a story. It's time to share it with the world—one video at a time.

A SMALL ASK...

If you found *YouTube for Authors* helpful, I'd be incredibly grateful if you would take a moment to leave an honest review.

You can leave a review wherever you purchased or downloaded the book, or visit DaleLinks.com/ReviewYouTubeBook to find the quickest way to share your feedback.

Here's why your review matters:

- **It helps other authors and creators know this book is worth their time.** When someone is deciding whether or not to pick up a new resource, real feedback from real readers makes all the difference.
- **It directly supports my work.** Reviews don't affect sales rankings, but they build trust, encourage new readers to give the book a chance, and help the author community grow stronger.

Even just leaving a star rating—no written review necessary—makes a huge difference.

Every bit of feedback helps authors like me continue creating resources that serve you better.

Thank you for being part of this journey, for supporting indie publishing, and for helping more authors discover the tools they need to succeed.

ABOUT THE AUTHOR

Dale L. Roberts is a bestselling author, publishing strategist, and relentless advocate for indie authors. With over 50 published titles and 43 literary awards, he's helped thousands of writers turn their passion into sustainable careers. As the founder of the *Self-Publishing with Dale* YouTube channels—now collectively boasting more than 120,000 subscribers—Dale has become one of the most trusted voices in the self-publishing space.

A former fitness author who built his brand from the ground up, Dale combines real-world publishing experience with a no-fluff, results-driven mindset. Whether you're launching your first book or scaling your author business, Dale delivers the tools, strategies, and tough-love motivation to help you succeed on your terms.

Relevant links:

- Website – SelfPublishingWithDale.com
- YouTube – YouTube.com/SelfPublishingWithDale
- YouTube Podcast – YouTube.com/@SelfPubWithDale

- My Books – DaleLinks.com/Bookshelf
- Discord – DaleLinks.com/Discord
- Twitter – X.com/SelfPubWithDale
- Facebook – Facebook.com/SelfPubWithDale

WANT MORE SUPPORT LIKE THIS?

If you found this book helpful, you'll love what I send to my email subscribers. Every week, I share practical tips, real-time updates, and behind-the-scenes insights to help indie authors grow their platforms and sell more books, without burning out.

Whether you're just starting out or already building momentum, these emails are designed to keep you informed, encouraged, and one step ahead of the curve.

And as a thank-you for joining, you'll also get instant access to my free **Bestseller Book Launch Checklist** to help you stay focused and consistent.

Join the list and grab your checklist at **DaleLinks.com/Checklist**

SPECIAL THANKS

First and foremost, my deepest, most heartfelt thank you goes to my wife and best friend, Kelli. You are truly the love of my life, and none of this would've been possible without you.

Next, a humongous thank you to every viewer who's watched even a fraction of a second of my content. Because of you, I've had the privilege of building a massive platform. Could I have found success without YouTube? Probably, but I believe all roads would've eventually led here. Who knows, maybe I'd have launched a fitness channel and sold even more of my exercise books.

Still, I wouldn't trade this journey for anything. My love for publishing far outgrew my fading interest in fitness. I hope you've felt that passion throughout this book and gained enough insight to start your YouTube journey today. My greatest wish is to see you succeed far beyond anything I've accomplished on the platform.

Finally, special thanks to Ava Fails, Bill Latoria, Shanon "S.D." Huston, and—most of all—Jeanne De Vita. You've all helped shape my work in ways that gave me confidence to keep publishing. One of the greatest gifts an author can receive is an inner circle that brings out their very best. I hope everyone finds a few people like these four in their own lives. You'll find more about these amazing folks in the Resources section. Buy a book or order a service, I know they'll appreciate it!

RESOURCES

Throughout this book, I've mentioned tools, platforms, books, and creators that have helped me succeed on YouTube and in my author business. Rather than clutter the reading experience with hyperlinks, I've gathered all the relevant links here in one easy-to-navigate list. Personally, I prefer clean digital reading without accidentally tapping a hyperlink, so this format keeps things simple while still giving you exactly what you need.

The list is organized in alphabetical order by name or product. Some links are affiliate links, which means I may earn a small commission if you choose to purchase or sign up through them. This comes at no extra cost to you. I only recommend tools and services I use myself and fully believe in.

BOOKS & COURSES

- *Infestate* by Dale Lewis Roberts – DaleLinks.com/Infestate
- *Sponsor Magnet* by Justin Moore – DaleLinks.com/SponsorMagnet
- *Tube Ritual* by Brian G. Johnson – DaleLinks.com/TubeRitual

- *Wide Publishing for Authors* by Dale L. Roberts – DaleLinks.com/WideBook

TOOLS, SOFTWARE & SERVICES

- ChatGPT – Chat.OpenAI.com
- Dibbly Create – DaleLinks.com/DibblyCreate
- eCamm – DaleLinks.com/eCamm
- Flocksy – DaleLinks.com/Flocksy
- Linktree – Linktr.ee
- MorningFame – DaleLinks.com/Morningfame
- TubeBuddy – DaleLinks.com/TubeBuddy
- VidIQ – DaleLinks.com/VidIQ

LIVESTREAMING & VIDEO PRODUCTION

- Restream – DaleLinks.com/Restream
- Streamyard – DaleLinks.com/Streamyard
- YouTube Studio – Studio.YouTube.com

YOUTUBE CREATORS & CHANNELS

- Brian G. Johnson – YouTube.com/BrianGJohnsonTV
- Creator Insider – YouTube.com/@CreatorInsider
- Creator Wizard – YouTube.com/@CreatorWizard
- Derral Eves – YouTube.com/@DerralEves
- Nick Nimmin – YouTube.com/NickNimmin
- Roberto Blake – Roberto Blake

- YouTube Insider (Rene Ritchie) – YouTube.com/@YouTubeInsider
- Walter Weyburn – YouTube.com/@WalterWeyburn

COLLABORATORS & ACKNOWLEDGMENTS

- Ava Fails – HeyYoAva.com
- Bill Latoria – DaleLinks.com/BillsBooks
- Jeanne De Vita – Book-Genie.com
- Shanon "S.D." Huston – YouTube.com/@SDHuston

MY REFERENCED VIDEOS

- My Reaction to Walter's gifted YouTube Play Button – Instagram.com/reel/CSxEgnRpy10
- *Book Rescue* (my video series) – BookRescueShow.com

REFERENCES

i	GMI Research Team. (2025 May 6). YOUTUBE STATISTICS 2025 (DEMOGRAPHICS, USERS BY COUNTRY & MORE). https://www.globalmediainsight.com/blog/youtube-users-statistics/

ii	Google. (2025 May 17). YouTube Partner Program overview & eligibility. https://support.google.com/youtube/answer/72851

iii	The Self-Publishing with Dale Podcast. (2022 August 11). Genius Level Book Marketing On TikTok | Brad Gosse. https://youtu.be/k4gNXwWtOFA?si=JD8DjSK_PCblO6F7

iv	Connell, A. (2025 January 1). 35 YouTube Shorts Statistics For 2025 (Growth & Trends). https://adamconnell.me/youtube-shorts-statistics/